Informed Learning

by Christine Susan Bruce

Association of College and Research Libraries
A division of the American Library Association
Chicago, 2008

The paper used in this publication meets the minimum requirements of American National Standard for Information Sciences-Permanence of Paper for Printed Library Materials, ANSI Z39.48-1992. ∞

Library of Congress Cataloging-in-Publication Data

Bruce, Christine.
  Informed learning / Christine Susan Bruce.
    p. cm.
  ISBN 978-0-8389-8489-5 (pbk. : alk. paper) 1. Learning. 2. Learning, Psychology of. 3. Motivation in education. 4. Interdisciplinary approach in education. 5. Education--Aims and objectives. I. Title.

  LB1060.B78 2008
  370.15--dc22

                        2008032707

Printed in the United States of America.

12 11 10 09 08   5 4 3 2 1

Table of Contents

Acknowledgements

For the inspiration for this book and for their tireless interest and contribution, I am indebted to dear colleagues who have worked closely with me and challenged me: Sylvia Edwards, Hilary Hughes, Mandy Lupton, Helen Partridge, and Ian Stoodley. I am also grateful for interaction over the years with many colleagues interested in information and its role in learning, especially Ross Todd, Louise Limberg, Sheila Webber, and Bill Johnston. Over the years, many conference committees and conveners of development programs have kindly invited me to speak and thus continued to challenge my thinking. More recently, others have generously corresponded with me about their work, especially Susie Andretta, Doug Colbeck, Clarence Maybee, and Mary Somerville. I would especially like to thank Mandy Lupton for her assistance with polishing the ideas for learning design and Hilary Hughes, Bill Johnston, Susie Andretta, and Jacqui Weetman da Costa for their attention to parts of the manuscript.

Informed learning is simultaneously about information use and learning. I am deeply grateful to several mentors and colleagues who inspired my early interest in learning, especially Phil Candy and Rod Gerber, Ference Marton, Lars Dahlgren, and Lennart Svensson. On the information side, leaders in the Queensland University of Technology Library made possible my early work with information use and learning, especially Tom Cochrane, Janice Rickards, and Jan Novak. In other parts of the world, Nancy Fjällbrant and Patricia Breivik motivated my interest in information literacy education.

Most important, my family has supported me inexhaustibly throughout the writing process.

All the summaries of research outcomes included throughout the book have been adapted by me from the authors' original work to highlight the interest of those studies to the informed learning agenda. These summaries are all considerably reduced versions of the full descriptions available from the cited sources. The material about the Six Frames of Informed Learning in chapter 2 has been adapted with permission from

Susie Andretta, the editor of the journal issue in which the material was originally published.

The original sources for the Six Frames and Seven Faces of Informed Learning were published by Auslib Press, Adelaide, Australia (info@aulib.com.au). Dr. Alan Bundy has been a leading advocate in Australia for the convergence of information use and learning. His special interest in the relational approach to information use and learning has made widely available the work of the Queensland University of Technology information literacy research team and the thinking of many other leaders in the field.

Preface

Once upon a time a little girl drew a picture of a teddy bear, which she called Rosie. Rosie's fur reflected the colors of the rainbow; Rosie sat on a canvas chair beside the beach, with the sun shining, grass growing, and a spider spinning a web alongside a brightly colored beach ball. When I looked at the picture, I asked the little girl what information she had used to create the picture. She was most puzzled. "But there are no words in the picture, Mummy," she said.

The little girl had already come to believe that text and information were closely related. So I tried again: "What do you know about that helped you make the picture?" This time she gave a different response. "Well, first of all there's Rosie," she said, picking up her teddy bear and giving her a hug. "Last holidays we went to the beach, and the spider came out of Charlotte's Web. The grass is growing outside, and how I put it together was my imagination."

This little girl was engaged in informed learning. She was using information of different kinds—physical, tangible objects, memories, and other things—to create something new. If she remembers my questions and thinks about them, as little girls can naturally be expected to do, she may come to understand her creative act as an act of information use, to see inspiration and information as related, and to recognize the importance of feeding her imagination. She may even come to appreciate how the processes apply to other pursuits. Will her teachers encourage her along the path of informed learning?

Welcome to *Informed Learning*. If you have opened this book, it is probably because you are interested in how people learn. It may also be because you are interested in how learners interact with their information environment and would like to help them do so in ways that help them learn better. What should we teach and how, so that our students will use information successfully, creatively and responsibly in their journey as lifelong learners?

Informed Learning provides a unique perspective on helping students become successful learners in our rapidly evolving information environments. It presents a new framework for informed learning that will enable teachers, librarians, researchers and teacher-researchers to work together as they continue to respond to the need to help students use information to learn.

Do you want to help your students engage with the information practices of their discipline or chosen profession? Are you looking for ideas to invigorate and refresh your curriculum? Are you looking for ways to help your students write better essays or search the internet more successfully? Are you looking for strategies to enhance your research supervision? Are you trying to discover how information literacy and information literacy education can contribute to academic curriculum? *Informed Learning* can help you.

Informed learning is using information, creatively and reflectively, in order to learn. It is learning that draws on the different ways in which we use information in academic, professional and community life, and it is learning that draws on emerging understandings of our varied experiences of using information to learn.

Indeed, we cannot learn without using information. The foundation of this book is problemetizing the interdependence between information use and learning. Most of the time, we take for granted the aspect of learning that we call information use. What might happen to the learning experience if we attend to it?

Informed Learning examines research into the experience of using information to learn in academic, workplace, and community contexts, research that can be used to inform learning and learning design at many levels. It draws on contemporary higher-education teaching and learning theory to suggest ways forward to build a learning agenda that values the need for engaging with the wider world of information. In doing so, it offers a new and unified framework for implementing curriculum that recognizes the importance of successful, creative, and reflective information use as a strategy for learning as well as a learning outcome, and it proposes a research agenda that will continue to inform learning.

Informed Learning reconceptualizes information literacy as being about engaging in information practices in order to learn, engaging with the different ways of using information to learn. Based on my work in developing the Seven Faces of Information Literacy, it proposes that teaching and learning must (a) bring about new ways of experiencing and using information, and (b) engage students with the information practices that are relevant to their discipline or profession.

This book is written for a diverse audience of educators from many disciplines, curriculum designers, researchers, and administrators. While this book establishes both a new approach to learning design and an associated research agenda, it is also intended to be practical. I have sought to ground the ideas in practice through

- using Steve and Jane, hypothetical academics from different disciplines who are on a journey experiencing the implementation of informed learning;
- using examples from the literature and personal experience;
- using reflective questions towards the end of each chapter.

In this book you will find many examples of how people experience information use as they go about learning in different contexts. The research reported here shows that as people go learn, they interact with information in different ways. They may be learning about a content area in a formal context, they may be engaged in informal learning as they go about their work and everyday lives, or they may be learning through doing original research.

The emphasis on experience and ways of seeing comes from the work of researchers into student learning such as Ference Marton, Paul Ramsden, Shirley Booth, Michael Prosser, Keith Trigwell, and others who have shown that, if we are to help students learn, we must first be aware of how they experience those aspects of the world about which they are learning.

Different Ways of Reading This Book

The first three chapters of this book establish the broad theoretical framework for informed learning, and the remaining chapters consider the outworkings of this framework in a range of contexts.

Based on your interests, you may want to read this book in different ways:

- If you want to browse the general directions of this book, read the narratives at the start of each chapter.
- If you want to see how the book might influence your practice, read the narratives and the reflective questions at the end of each chapter.

- If you want to help your students become informed learners in their discipline or profession, focus on chapters 1, 2, 3, and 5.
- If you are looking for help with students engaged in information practices such as Internet searching or essay writing, focus on chapters 1, 3, and 4.
- If you are interested in informed learning in the community or workplace, focus on chapters 1, 2, 3, and 6.
- If you want to help your research students become informed learners, focus on chapters 1, 2, 3, 7, and 8.
- If you are working with colleagues to promote information literacy education and are looking for ideas, read chapter 9.
- If you are interested in researching informed learning, read chapter 10.

Overview of the Content of Individual Chapters

Chapter 1—Informed Learning

This chapter develops the idea of informed learning. I identify the key concepts associated with informed learning and the agendas that have contributed to its emergence. I also describe informed learning as under-pinned by information practices and consider our ways of experiencing information and information use as being critical elements of informed learning. In this chapter, I explore the relationship between learning and information use, establishing that content is learned through effective interaction with information and also that (a) learners' views of, and approaches to, the content of learning appear to influence information use, and (b) learners' approach to information use appears to influence the content of learning. We can help our students become informed learners by introducing into the curriculum explicit attention to infor-mation practices.

Chapter 2—Six Frames for Informed Learning

Informed learning draws from what we know about variation in the experience of learning and teaching. In this chapter, I explore how the idea of informed learning may be approached differently in the curricu-lum depending on the conceptions of learning, information, and other dimensions adopted by those involved. The Six Frames for Informed Learning identify several dimensions that may vary depending on the personal experiences and view of those involved, including approach to assessment, information use, teaching, learning, information, and content.

Chapter 3—Seven Faces of Informed Learning
Informed learning draws from our understanding of how we use information as we go about learning. In this chapter, I explore the Seven Faces of Informed Learning as a transdisciplinary model of learning through engagement with information. The Seven Faces of Informed Learning is a model that underpins most applications of information practices in academic settings. It is a relational model, developed through investigating people's experiences and contributing to the Relational frame for informed learning, one of the Six Frames described in chapter 2. Selected examples show how the faces may be applied to the design of learning tasks and to invigorate curriculum.

Chapter 4—Students' Experiences of Informed Learning
The theory of informed learning draws from our understanding of students' experiences of using information to learn. Applying the theory to help students become better at using information to learn begins with understanding their experience of informed learning. In this chapter, I examine information use from the students' perspective, how they use information as they go about learning. I then review insights into students' experiences of specific information practices that influence learning, such as essay writing, assignment writing, and Internet searching that are of interest across disciplines and cohorts. In the latter part of the chapter, I explore strategies for encouraging reflection to bring about learning.

Chapter 5—Informed Learning in the Disciplines and Professions
Informed learning is grounded in disciplinary and professional information practices. In this chapter, I review research into information use in discipline-specific and professional contexts. The chapter opens with academics' perspectives of information literacy in specific disciplines. It then explores different experiences of information literacy and use in specific professions. Senior managers' experiences of information literacy, views of use of the Internet for information sharing in the

construction industry, and the information practices of auditors all contribute to the growing picture of the informed learning experience. The chapter goes on to explore the diverse experience of information in a range of disciplines and provides examples of curriculum design.

Chapter 6—Informed Learning in the Community and Workplace
Using information to learn is central not only in the academic context, but also in the workplace and community. As we extend students' learning experiences into workplace and community contexts, students have the opportunity to come to experience or reflect on informed learning in those settings. In this chapter, I introduce the GeST windows for considering informed learning in the workplace and the community. I explore the character of informed learning in these settings, adapting the Seven Faces model to suggest what the experience of informed learning might look like in those settings. This chapter invites exploration of what it might mean to prepare students to be informed learners in the community or workplace and to respond to workplace and community issues in their professional practice.

Chapter 7—Informed Learning in the Research Community
This chapter explores the idea of informed learning in the research community and its applicability to research degree study and supervision. It mirrors the early chapters' examination of what we know about the experience of using information to learn. In this chapter, I review developments in uncovering the experience of research, examine the notion of Six Frames for Informed Learning in the context of learning to research, and adapt the Seven Faces of Informed Learning to the research setting. I focus primarily on researchers and what we know of academic experiences in that role. Towards the end of the chapter, I make some suggestions about possible relationships between information use and research.

Chapter 8—Research Higher-Degree Students and Informed Learning
In this chapter, I explore informed learning in the research higher-degree context. It opens with an overview of how research is experienced by students. The idea of informed learning itself is envisioned from a research student's perspective. The literature review is explored as an

example of an information practice that is experienced differently by research students. Different ways of experiencing the literature review itself and the scope of the literature review are described. Reflective strategies for expanding students' experience are suggested.

Chapter 9—Championing Informed Learning Across the Organization
What conditions need to be put into place for informed learning to thrive? How can different members of the university community work together to promote informed learning? In this chapter, I explore how we might influence a university, raising awareness of informed learning. I propose RACER as an approach to bringing about curriculum change. RACER identifies five points of focus:

- Recognize different roles and perspectives
- Accept diversity
- Change with support
- Engage in the scholarship of teaching
- Research the future

I then look at how the Six Frames and Seven Faces models might be used for academic development and highlight disciplinary perspectives on information literacy pedagogy.

Chapter 10—Informed Learning: A Research Agenda
The idea of informed learning has taken form through problemetizing using information for learning and through applying the idea that learning is about experiencing variation to that problem area in a sustained way. Implementation and ongoing development of informed learning rests on furthering our understanding of using information to learn in different contexts. What are the information practices that enable ongoing learning in the work of the different professions, the information practices that enable people to learn with and from each other? What are the information practices that underpin the many disciplines being taught and learned? What are the forms of information engaged with, and how are they used? In this chapter, I propose a research agenda that may be contributed to by members of all disciplines, by researchers in the fields of information literacy, information, and learning.

Chapter 1

Informed Learning

Opening Narrative

Jane and Steve are new academics who come to the university after several years of professional practice. Steve is an artist, and Jane is an engineer. In conversation one afternoon, they realize that they both want their students to be able to keep learning after the students complete their courses. How can they design learning experiences to meet this goal?

Steve believes that it is important for artists to explore the work of other artists, to recognize and be in touch with whatever might inspire art, and to journal or document the ongoing journey in some way. Steve asks his students to form learning circles to share their explorations and inspirations each week and to collate an electronic portfolio recording their learning.

Jane asks her students to work towards a student-managed conference for which they will write and present their own papers, invite key industry players and researchers as keynote speakers, and publish the proceedings of the day on the Web.

*Both Steve and Jane have **identified key information practices** in their profession and found ways of integrating those practices into the learning experience.*

*These practices reflect some of the ways in which informed learning is experienced in their professional areas. In the two cases, **the information is very different**—visual, oral, or textual. In both cases, their students need to engage in some aspect of informed learning—using technology for awareness or communication, identifying sources of relevant information, organizing information, developing their personal knowledge bases, and using the information acquired with wisdom or professional judgment.*

*Jane and Steve are engaging their students in relevant information practices. By sharing the character of informed learning with students and inviting students to reflect on what they have learned about information use in the professional context, Jane and Steve will enhance their students' professional capabilities with information. Their students are on their way to reaping the benefits of **informed learning**.*

1

This chapter develops the idea of informed learning. I first identify the key concepts associated with informed learning and the agendas that have contributed to its emergence. I also describe informed learning as being underpinned by information practices and discuss our ways of experiencing information and information use as being critical elements of informed learning. In this chapter, I explore the relationship between learning and information use, establishing that content is learned through effective interaction with information. I also establish that (a) learners' views of, and approaches to, the content of learning appear to influence information use, and (b) learners' approach to information use appears to influence the content of learning. We can help our students become informed learners by introducing into our curriculum explicit attention to using information.

What Is Informed Learning?

This book is about how we interact with and use information as we learn: learning formally through studying or doing research at universities, and learning informally in community and work contexts. It is about the experience of informed learning, examining how students, teachers, and researchers use information as they go about learning through coursework and research. It is about empowering learners to continue to learn in the many facets of their lives.

It is also about how we see ourselves as informed learners, about how we see our information practices and the ideas that inform our practices. It is about how we can help students become informed learners by introducing them to the difference facets of informed learning. It is about the importance of understanding informed learning in the community and workplace as part of the professional journeys of all of us.

When we ask students to use information to learn, we can help them to become more creative, reflective, and successful information users. For example, a teacher may require students to prepare a variety of communications about the impact of global warming. Her students may use a wide range of information sources, including media sources, research databases, Web sites, and blogs, as well as interviewing members of the local community. They may establish a position regarding the diverse viewpoints on the topic and be able to communicate what they have learned to different audiences. This teacher is asking students to use information to learn. She can enhance their learning by helping them to understand, improve, and expand their own experience of informed learning and by encouraging them to use information in ways that reflect those of experts in the field.

Informed learning:

- is using information to learn;
- draws on the different ways in which we use information in academic, professional, and community life;
- draws on understandings of our varied experiences of using information to learn;
- is informed by academic and professional information practices (the regular activities we undertake within which we use information);
- is informed by an understanding of how such practices are experienced;
- is about how we interact with information while learning;
- is about how we use information to learn;
- is about the information and knowledge-construction practices that are relevant to discipline-centered curriculum;
- is about the creative, reflective, and ethical use of information for learning.

In today's information-rich society, high-quality interaction with the information environment is the cornerstone of all learning. By being creative and reflective information users, we are able to learn and to continue learning in any field or walk of life. As educators, we need to think about information use and its relationship with learning when we design learning. We need to emphasize both discipline and information-use outcomes in our learning design and implementation; discipline mastery is achieved through the processes of creative and reflective information use. Once we recognize what information is and how we are using it, we can be more in charge of the information environment and how we encounter, source, control, engage with, and use information. We cannot assume that learners are aware of these processes or that they are able to implement them. The learning experience that prepares today's students for tomorrow's professional practice brings such practices into the curriculum and encourages reflection upon them.

Informed learning requires us to pay closer attention to the experience of using information to learn. Informed learning promotes learning through effective engagement with information. It brings to our attention the information practices that bring about learning and draws on our understanding of the experience of informed learning to improve the quality of learning. Informed learning attends simultaneously to the content and context of learning (the discipline-focused outcomes) and to information use, including relevant professional and disciplinary practices.

Informed learning makes it possible for learners to experience information use in its diverse forms. Informed learning brings into the curriculum information practices and insights into the experience of information use. It draws on workplace and community information practices, as well as the information practices prevalent in the academic and professional communities.

Informed learning involves experiencing information practices and making explicit learning about those practices via a process of reflection, enabling transfer of learning process to new contexts. In doing so informed learning helps students walk the path of lifelong learning.

The keys to informed learning are experiences of information use, the experiences of all learners—students, teachers, researchers, and other information users. The adoption and implementation of informed learning require that we understand the perceptual worlds of learners as information users.

Where Does the Idea of Informed Learning Come From?

The idea of informed learning comes from recognizing that information use and learning are close companions; in formal learning environments, discipline content and effective information use need to be learned together as interrelated phenomena. I have devised the concept of informed learning by bringing together an evolving research base, described in this book that explores the experience of using information to learn among academics and students in professional practice and in the community.

In my involvement with the information literacy agenda (for an overview of this important agenda, see Horton, 2007), I have come to see that the term *information literacy* is often used to represent many concepts that should be recognized as separate. For example, information literacy and information literacy education are separate concepts, in the same way that science and science education, or art and art education, are separate concepts. Similarly, informed learning and information literacy are separate ideas, in the same way that problem-based learning and problem solving are separate concepts.

At present, the terms *information literacy* and *information literacy education* continue to be understood in some places as being about the acquisition of technological skills, library skills, and information skills, while elsewhere they are used to refer to the experience of using information as we go about learning. All these skills are necessary, but sometimes we stop with the skills and do not focus on how students and others must use information to learn. Confining information literacy to such skills denies learners the rich potential that may be gained from broader attention to the different ways of experiencing information use in the disciplines, professions, and community.

When we see information literacy as a complex of different ways of using information to learn, we open the door to informed learning. Informed learning brings learner-centered, experiential, and reflective approaches to the information literacy agenda. Informed learning provides the language and the organizing concept that allow us to focus on understanding and improving students' use of information as they learn.

Towards a Common Understanding of the Key Terms Used in This Book

There are many concepts used in this book that appear closely related and are sometimes difficult to distinguish. Below I identify several of these key concepts and define the terms that I use. A more extended set of terms is included in chapter 10.

- **Informed learning**: using information to learn.
- **Information**: anything that we experience as informing. Information will appear differently in different contexts and different disciplines.
- **Learning**: coming to experience the world in new ways.
- **Information literacy**: experiencing different ways of using information to learn.

- **Information skills**: the building blocks that make information literacy possible, in the same way that the ability to read and write makes literate practice possible.

As a way of highlighting the differences in their meaning, Table 1.1 compares the concepts of informed learning with the concepts associated with problem-based learning, a different agenda that may be familiar to readers. Some readers may find it easier to see the difference between informed learning and information literacy when they compare it with the difference between problem-based learning and problem-solving ability. The latter two concepts stand in the same relationship to each other as do the former. In this book, I do not explore any relationship between informed learning and problem-based learning, although such a relationship may indeed be possible. Problem-based learning is used here simply as a counterpoint to reveal more clearly the nuances in the informed learning agenda.

Table 1.1 Comparing basic concepts associated with informed learning against concepts associated with problem-based learning

Informed learning is using information to learn.	**Problem-based learning** is solving problems to learn.
Information literacy is being able to draw upon different ways of experiencing the use of information to learn.	**Problem-solving ability** is being able to draw upon different ways of experiencing problem solving.
Information practices are the practical processes and contexts within which information is used, for example, professional development, essay writing, and research.	**Problem-solving practices** are the processes through which problems are solved, for example, conducting interviews and research.
Information is anything we experience as informing.	**A problem** is anything we experience as unresolved.
Information skills are the building blocks that make information literacy possible, for example, database search and creation skills, referencing skills, computer skills, and library skills.	**Problem-solving skills** are the building blocks that make problem solving possible, for example, numerical skills, communications skills, interviewing skills, analysis skills, and creativity.

What Are the Characteristics of Informed Learning?

- Informed learning draws from our understanding of the experience of learning and teaching. It is supported by research into student learning and different ways of experiencing teaching and assessment.
- Informed learning draws from our understanding of the experience of using information to learn. Informed learning draws from insights into the experience of information literacy and information use among students, academics, teachers, and researchers, as well as in the community and workplace.
- Informed learning brings the different ways of using information to learn to students' attention. Informed learning seeks to expand the repertoire of students' experiences and to help them adopt the full range of possible experiences.
- Informed learning is grounded in the information practices of academic disciplines or professions. Informed learning is dynamic, flexible, and creative, mirroring real-life experiences. Its character reflects the disciplines in which it is experienced.
- Informed learning brings information practices and the different ways of experiencing them to students' attention.
- Informed learning considers information use and professional information practices at the same time as the content. It underpins independent and collaborative learning. Informed learning supports innovation and evidence-based practice. It fosters intuition and understanding. Information use for informed learning is fundamentally critical, creative, reflective, and ethical. It encourages students to reflect on aspects of information use and information practices, including what they have learned about their discipline or profession through such practices.
- Informed learning accepts the diverse forms that information might take. It engages students with the kinds of information that are important to their disciplinary or professional practice and ensures an appreciation of the context from which information has been created or derived. Information may take the form of pictures, sound, or text; it may be static or moving; it may be two- or three-dimensional. It may take the form of research outcomes or community discourse.
- Informed learning supports social engagement and development, cultural understandings, social networking, community and peer

support (including volunteer), shared learning, and communicative learning. Informed learning is transformative. It has the potential to bring about change in the way that students see themselves, their profession, and their professional practice. Informed learning is empowering; it brings about personal and social development.

• Informed learning is balanced. It can redress the imbalance between students' digital competence and their less-developed critical awareness. Informed learning may or may not engage new ICTs (information and communication technologies). While up-to-date ICTs are an advantage, the real priority is engagement with information: creative, reflective, and transformational information use.

• Informed learning is socially responsible. It supports wise use of information, recognizes rights and responsibilities of information use, respects intellectual property, and supports online security and safety.

• Informed learning is a shared responsibility among discipline educators, content experts, information and ICT professionals, industry, and the community.

What Are Information Practices?

Information practices are those academic, professional, and civic activities that require interaction with the information environment; sometimes within a technological context and sometimes not. Much of what we do as professionals, students, and researchers in all disciplines takes the form of an information practice. Whether we are making decisions, seeking new knowledge, writing for a grade or a publication, preparing a report for a client, developing a Web page, composing music, or programming new software, we are engaged in an information practice. As we learn through our encounters with information, as we seek out information, work with information, and give others the benefit of our learning, we are engaged in important learning processes in today's information and knowledge contexts.

Some of the academic information practices that may inform learning are keeping up-to-date in the field; writing essays; participating in journal clubs, workshops, conferences, and symposia; making decisions; seeking new knowledge; writing for a grade or for publication; and searching the Internet. These practices allow us to learn content through the process of information use. Information practices rely on creative, reflective, and ethical information use. How information use, in a general sense, is experienced in the academic environment, the workplace, and the community is the topic of chapters 3 and 6.

Some of the professional and discipline information practices that already influence learning include broad processes such as evidence-based practice, design, problem solving, and research, as well as specific tasks such as preparing a report for a client, developing a Web page, composing music, or programming new software. Individual disciplines and professions will have specific practices that belong to them. Professional and discipline-specific practices are discussed in chapter 5.

Sample Engagements Blending Information Interactions and Content Learning

Each of these activities could be undertaken in online, blended, or traditional learning environments:

- Individuals or groups could design a strategy for maintaining professional or research currency and discuss what is learned through the implementation of that strategy over time.
- Individuals or groups could develop a package of materials for a client and prepare a covering statement about how the information was gathered, how they assess the quality of the information, and how that information might be used by the client.
- A class group could review existing information on a current topic and develop a series of journal articles or conference papers to inform each other or external audiences.
- "Reading groups" focused on a key text or series of texts could be formed, in which students repeatedly address key questions about the content of the text to deepen their understanding of the field. "Journal clubs," in which students share and interpret current articles on a topic of interest, may achieve similar ends.
- Students could work in teams to research and create a learning resource for the unit's learning community and critique other teams' resources.

Why Attend to Academic and Professional Information Practices in Designing Learning?

From a pragmatic perspective, we need to simply improve the quality of learning. Practically speaking, there are internal and external imperatives to meet institutional and quality assurance requirements. In this context, there are a range of issues we as educators may be concerned with, including the need to

- prepare students for independent, informal learning at work as well as in civic and personal life;
- help students work in innovative learning contexts, for example, inquiry, problem-based, or action learning;
- equip students to learn in ever-changing information and technology environments;
- meet the requirements of accrediting bodies, professional associations, and employers;
- satisfy both "earner-learners" and those seeking a liberal education;
- develop intercultural perspectives for academic, professional, community, or social learning in global environments.

Whatever our reasons, we need to remember that using information creatively, reflectively, and ethically to interact confidently with our ever-changing information environment is not a prerequisite to learning. It is a learning strategy that belongs to all disciplines at all levels and that can be explicitly designed into the learning experience to benefit those being prepared to enter the field. Learners should be introduced to the forms of information practice that are prevalent in the disciplines or professions they are studying.

Many educators already include information practices in their learning design. Most learner-centered approaches to curriculum design, such as inquiry learning or problem-based learning, rely on individuals or teams engaging in information practices. Research students and researchers are heavily engaged in information practices as a matter of course.

Teaching for Informed Learning

Informed learning is based not only on drawing upon information practices to bring about learning, but also on the idea that informed learning, and the information practices in which information literacy finds expression, can be experienced in different ways. This is the key to the Relational frame for informed learning described in chapter 2.

In the Relational frame, we as teachers and our students experience those things that we are learning in different ways. Our different experiences are a result of seeing or looking at the world differently; further, we see differently because we are focusing our attention on particular aspects of those things we are teaching or learning. In this approach, teaching is helping learners to see the world differently by focusing their attention on relevant parts. Chapters 3 through 8 provide many examples of how we focus differently in our experiences of information use and how our different experiences may be used in learning design.

This way of thinking about teaching and learning has been developed and described by Marton and Booth (1997). They propose a *pedagogy of awareness*, in which powerful ways of seeing lead to powerful ways of acting. When we see some part of the world in a particular way, we could say that we are wearing a particular set of lenses (Edwards, 2006). These lenses establish what we are paying close attention to, or focusing on. They also establish what is more in the background of our awareness, what we are not attending to closely. These ways of seeing are often referred to in the research literature as *conceptions*.

Revisiting the paragraphs above will reveal that I commenced with writing about experiences and concluded with writing about ways of seeing and the lenses through which we see. This is because the word experience emphasizes the meanings that we associate with the things we are learning, and *ways of seeing*, or the *lenses through which we see*, emphasizes the structures through which we derive those meanings.

Marton and Booth's (1997) pedagogy of awareness suggests that learning occurs when we become aware of the different lenses through which we might see the object of our learning. The intention is to bring about a qualitative change in the way learners see, experience, understand, or conceptualize something, rather than changing the amount of knowledge they possess. Indeed, knowledge is considered to be about discerning the world in particular ways. For example, music is learned when different sounds are discerned; reading is learned when the relationship between written words and spoken sounds is discerned; information use is learned when different ways of experiencing it are discerned; information searching is learned when different ways of experiencing that are discerned. For example, in relation to information searching, consider the difference between searching while understanding the structure of a database and searching without understanding the structure; you will appreciate the powerful influence of structure on searching. Bringing about learning through widening experience, and thus revealing variation, is the underlying principle. This way of thinking about learning is also now known as *variation theory* (Marton & Tsui, 2004).

A considerable amount of research into teaching and learning has been conducted using this approach, including the subset of studies, drawn together in this book that shed light on informed learning. In each of these studies, the outcome is a series of ways of seeing the concept or activity in question. In some studies, the different ways of seeing range from simple to complex; in some, they are simply different; and in other studies, some ways of seeing are considered better than others for various reasons. Such studies make available a research base that can inform teachers' professional judgment in determining which experiences are important for their students.

What Are the Principles of Informed Learning?

Informed Learning Takes Into Account Learners' Experiences
The power of informed learning comes from bringing to students' attention the character of informed learning and helping them to reflect on their own capacity to learn as they engage with information. Within the context of informed learning this means

- developing a picture of students' experiences of informed learning;
- building into curriculum relevant experiences that will encourage them to adopt the desired experiences;
- building reflection on those experiences into curriculum;
- making it possible for students to apply their experience to novel contexts (adapted from Bruce, 2002).

Informed Learning Promotes the Simultaneous Development of Discipline and Process Learning
In order to promote the simultaneous development of discipline and process learning, we need to have a sense of how our students are experiencing both information use and the content they are learning. Learners

need to use information practices appropriate to their discipline or field of study and to be equipped with the appropriate lenses to help them use information powerfully. They also need to be learning discipline content as they work with information. Students should be learning about something (discipline content) as they engage in learning to use information; coming to see both the content and the information use in more powerful ways. This assumes that content is learned through effective interaction with information. Informed learning is not about mastering a skill set, but rather "a process that should transform both learning and the culture of communities for the better" (Breivik, 2000).

Informed Learning Is About Changes in Experience
If learning is about coming to see the world in new or more complex ways (Marton & Booth, 1997), then learning to be an information-empowered professional, researcher, or scientist is about developing new and more complex ways of experiencing informed learning. As teachers, we need to help students develop new and more complex ways of working with information, helping them to be informed learners. From a discipline perspective, this may relate to their understanding of particular topic areas or to the wider discipline. From the information-use perspective, this may relate to their experience of the information practice, the tool, or what they are willing to admit to their information universe (see the following section, On the Relationship Between Using Information and Learning).

In the following chapters of this book, I will show how we can apply these principles by investigating the experience of informed learning and then by designing learning to strengthen informed learning in university contexts.

On the Relationship Between Using Information and Learning

Most of us who design learning experiences around information practices do so because we know or believe that these practices bring about learning. Research is now showing us that there is a unique relationship between information literacy, which finds expression in information practices, and learning; information use is an important mediator in the learning process. We have growing evidence of an interrelationship between learners' experience of the content of learning and their experience of using information to learn. Because the experience of information use influences learning in several ways, attending to aspects of the information literacy experience becomes an important strategy in helping us to influence learning. Insights into the relationship between information use and learning are emerging as follows:

• *Students' experiences of information seeking are related to their learning outcomes.* For example, Louise Limberg (2000) demonstrates the relationship between learners' different ways of seeking and using information and the depth of understanding they achieve about the topic being studied (see chapter 4).

• *Students' experiences of academic information practices are related to their information-use processes and approaches to learning.* For example, Mandy Lupton (2004) shows how students' approaches to essay writing are closely associated with the ways in which they use information in their course of study and also closely associated with their understanding of what they are doing when learning. Sylvia Edwards (2006) demonstrates that university students are likely to search the Internet in different ways; the more sophisticated searchers are aware of their research topic, the structure of the information environment, and the quality of the information they are engaging with, taking a more fruitful approach to their learning (see chapter 4).

• *Learners' views of their discipline are related to the extent of their information universe.* For example, recent research into learning to program at the introductory level suggests that students with more sophisticated views of the nature of programming experience a more complex information environment (see chapter 4).

• *How learners engage with information and what information they engage with depend on how they interpret the learning task.* For example, Lupton (2008) suggests that music students' experiences of composition are related to what they interpret information to be and how they work with that information. She also shows that students who perceive personal and professional relevance in their learning draw upon different forms of information and use the information in more complex ways (see chapter 4).

• *There is no apparent link between mastery of information-searching skills and the quality of students' information-use experience.* Sylvia Edwards (2006, p. 71) pre-tested students' library and database-searching skills before she investigated their experience of learning to search the Internet. She discovered that students' test scores were not a predictor of the quality of their searching. Students with high skills scores often took less critical and reflective approaches to Web searching.

• *Learners reflecting on information use are likely to improve the quality of their information-use processes.* Susie Andretta (2008) and Bill Johnston and Sheila Webber (2003) show that students who regularly reflect on information use adopt more sophisticated approaches to their work (see chapter 3).

• *Treating information seeking and information use as integrated processes promotes learning.* Studies by Louise Limberg (2000), Clarence Maybee (2006), and Christine Bruce (1997) suggest that seeing information seeking and information use as separate processes may lead to surface approaches to learning and impoverished learning outcomes, while seeing the two as interrelated and synergistic promotes more complex thinking. This is, in fact, the cornerstone of informed learning (see chapters 3 and 4).

As we have just seen, there is a growing body of evidence suggesting that information and information use could be regarded as mediators between learning intent and learning outcomes. If we understand information literacy as being about using information to learn, we can draw on information use or information practices to help secure the learning outcomes we seek. Information use becomes one dimension of the complex phenomenon we know as learning. Being aware of the role of information and its uses becomes an avenue for improving learning. Treating information use and learning as closely related enhances the learning experience.

ICTs and Informed Learning

The 21st-century higher-education learning context shares much in common with the professional context. At its heart are the twin foci of discipline concerns and professional practice. Transforming both are the information and communication technologies that have rapidly evolved in recent years.

The 20th century was dedicated to allowing technologies to influence teaching and learning. From the invention of radio, television, computers, the Internet, and the increasingly small mobile technologies, we have sought ways of using these technologies to reach learners in different places and to give flexibility to the learning experience. We have sought to create interactive and communicative virtual learning environments that replicate face-to-face classroom experiences, and we have developed new learning objects and contexts that only technology have made possible, for example, animations and videoconferencing.

Largely as a result of technology, discipline learning and professional practice take place in an increasingly information-rich environment and in an environment where professional and academic practices, including information practices, are increasingly transformed by new technologies. Communication with clients takes place via e-mail and the Web; journals are contributed to and read online; conferences are attended online; evidence for professional decisions is sought from a wide array of sources, including online hosts; brokers and other information professionals, especially librarians, play a vital role in ensuring the flow of reliable or high-quality information; professional meetings are conducted via chat groups. These are just a few examples of the *information practices* that sit at the heart of day-to-day learning and work in many professions in an online environment that continues to be chaotic. Particularly in social networking spaces, new phenomena such as blogs, wikis, Second Life, YouTube, and MySpace continue to change the ways in which we experience our virtual worlds.

In some cases, technology may make it harder for people to be informed learners. ICTs are important and influential but often do not provide solutions for those struggling to use the technologies. Today's digital or virtual environments make it harder for people to be "information savvy" (Lorenzo & Bziuban, 2006). The sheer volume of content and software available makes successful and creative use of what is available an ongoing challenge.

While many information practices are now inextricably entwined with technology, the conceptual skills involved transcend technology; the more complex forms of informed learning are less dependent on technology, and these practices must be privileged in order to ensure that when technology is available, it can be used to maximum advantage. For example, a writer must seek history, context, inspiration, collaboration, and review with or without technology. While technology may simplify the process or make it more complex, may act as a barrier or may add new facets to the experience, the basic practices remain. A scientist must understand how knowledge has developed in her field, who has contributed, what they have contributed, the potential nature of her own contribution, what constitutes scientifically acceptable knowledge and acceptable practices for generating that knowledge; a decision maker or problem solver must have the required heuristics to engage in those processes if technology is going to facilitate or enhance their experience. Again, technology may make a range of contributions: scientific information practices have evolved from scientific letter writing to the possibilities of e-research. Nevertheless, technology itself is powerless unless in the hands of an informed learner.

At the same time, we are aware that people need to be creative and reflective information users in both ICT-rich and ICT-poor contexts. While there are reasons why we might wish to provide access, lack of access to new technologies need not inhibit informed learning. We must avoid imposing the norms of information and ICT use that have evolved in developed and high-technology contexts. We must learn to understand the character of information that is considered important in different discipline, professional, community, and other contexts. We must bring the information practices of the many privileged and underprivileged communities we serve to the fore. We must learn to understand and facilitate the information practices of people of all genders, ages, cultures, and races.

Creative, reflective, and ethical information use brings about learning and is the foundation of the evolution of our future learning organizations and communities: in short, the evolution of our global future. As we build curriculum in formal contexts, we need to both prepare students for the learning organization and learning communities and prepare them to participate in and develop community information practices that empower all people.

How Is Informed Learning Achieved?

The prospect of informed learning requires the commitment of a wide academic community, including educators from all disciplines, researchers, industry partners, learning advisers, librarians, and other information and technology professionals. Partnerships are forged between members of these groups for many educational purposes. Such partnerships may be built upon, or new ones created, in support of informed learning. Schools and libraries have an important role in starting and helping people walk the informed learning journey.

As we have seen above, informed learning relies on educators attempting to establish the different ways of experiencing information literacy and information practices among their learners. Being able to do so may involve drawing from existing research, conducting classroom research, or seeking out our own professional insights and intuitions in this area. Once we have sought out variation, we are then in a position to encourage more appropriate experiences or to widen the range of students' experiences so that they may draw upon relevant experiences in future.

Clearly, the world of information use and learning is experienced in many different ways. How we as learners and educators experience aspects of our world has a profound influence on the character of our learning and our students' learning. Throughout this book, I address a number of key challenges we face as we attempt to give students curriculum experiences that will help them become learners, researchers, and practitioners, and become in their turn mentors and advocates in all walks of life:

• *First, the challenge of diverse ways of approaching informed learning in curriculum design.* The Six Frames for Informed Learning are the curriculum framework supporting informed learning, the different frames through which informed learning might be viewed. I examine the Six Frames to explore the different ways in which teaching and learning through the adoption of information practices can be approached by educators, students, and administrators (see chapter 2).

• *Second, the challenge of diverse ways of experiencing informed learning and information.* The Seven Faces of Informed Learning are the phenomenon underpinning informed learning, the experiences of using information to learn with which we want students to become familiar I examine the Seven Faces and some of the implications for how we might design learning experiences (see chapter 3).

• *Third, the challenge of adopting informed learning in coursework and research programs,* including an appreciation of informed learning in the community and workplace. While the distinction between coursework and research is somewhat artificial, I use it here to allow a special focus on students engaged in higher-degree research (see chapters 4, 5, 6, 7, and 8).

• *Fourth, the challenge of taking the informed learning agenda forward through staff development and cultural change.* I present the RACER approach for the successful implementation of informed learning programs as a framework for tackling key cultural issues and for revealing some of the complexities of a university's sociopolitical environment as we tackle the curriculum change agenda (see chapter 9).

• *Fifth, the challenge of taking forward, through research, the informed learning agenda* (see chapter 10).

Key Questions Arising From This Chapter—What Can We as Educators Do to Take This Agenda Further?

Each chapter in this book concludes with a few questions that may prompt us to think further about the key issues raised and implications for our contexts. Readers' contexts may involve diverse institutions or different student cohorts, perhaps with varying levels of expertise or varying cultural backgrounds. The questions are offered in the spirit of focusing attention on particular areas of the emerging informed learning agenda with a view to opening up a wider, systematic approach to research and scholarship in the area.

Informed Learning and Your Philosophy of Teaching
- Describe examples from your own experience that illustrate why informed learning is important for your students.
- Describe examples from your own experience that point towards the relationship between information use and learning.
- How might informed learning support your learning and teaching?

Informed Learning and Your Students
- Why might informed learning be important for your students?
- How might or do ICTs contribute to the experience of informed learning for your students?
- How might or do ICTs distract from the experience of informed learning for your students?

Informed Learning and Your Curriculum Practice
- What learning strategies are you already using that reflect the informed learning agenda?
- What is working well with these strategies, and what do you see as in need of improvement?
- Whom could you work with to take further steps towards informed learning?

Informed Learning in Your Field
- What are the important information practices in your discipline or profession?
- What learning strategies used in your discipline reflect the informed learning agenda?

References

Andretta, S. (2008, manuscript). Facilitating Information Literacy Education (FILE). In A. Brine (Ed.), *Handbook of library training practice and development (Vol. 3)*. Aldershot, UK: Gower Publishing.

Breivik, P. (2000). Foreword. In C. Bruce & P. Candy (Eds.), *Information literacy around the world: Advances in programs and research* (p. xi). Riverina, New South Wales, Australia: Centre for Information Studies, Charles Sturt University.

Bruce, C. S (1997). *The seven faces of information literacy*. Blackwood, South Australia: Auslib Press.

Bruce, C. S. (2002). Information literacy as a catalyst for educational change: A background paper. White paper prepared for UNESCO, the U.S. National Commission on Libraries and Information Science, and the National Forum on Information Literacy, for use at the Information Literacy, Meetings of Experts, Prague, The Czech Republic, September 2003 (pp. 1–17). [Retrieved October 7, 2006] from http://www.nclis.gov/libinter/infolitconf&meet/papers/bruce-fullpaper.pdf

Edwards, S. L. (2006). *Panning for gold: information literacy and the net lenses model*. Blackwood, South Australia: Auslib Press.

Horton, F. W. (2007). *Understanding information literacy: A primer*. Paris: United Nations Educational, Scientific, and Cultural Organisation.

Johnston, B., & Webber, S. (2003). Information literacy in higher education: A review and case study. *Studies in Higher Education, 28,* 335–352.

Limberg, L. (2000). Is there a relationship between information seeking and learning outcomes? In C. Bruce & P. Candy (Eds.), *Information literacy around the world: Advances in programs and research* (pp. 193–208).

Riverina, New South Wales, Australia: Centre for Information Studies, Charles Sturt University.

Lorenzo, G., & Bziuban, C. (2006). Ensuring the Net Generation is Net savvy. Educause Learning Initiative, September 2006, ID: ELI3006: 1–19.

Lupton, M. (2004). *The learning connection: Information literacy and the student experience.* Adelaide, South Australia: Auslib Press.

Lupton, M. (manuscript, 2008). *Information literacy and learning.* PhD thesis. Brisbane, Australia: Queensland University of Technology. (Final version to be available at http://adt.library.qut.edu.au)

Marton, F., & Booth, S. (1997). *Learning and awareness.* Mahwah, NJ: Erlbaum.

Marton, F., & Tsui, A. B. M. (2004). *Classroom discourse and the space of learning.* Mahwah, NJ: Erlbaum.

Maybee, C. (2006). Undergraduate perceptions of information use: The basis for creating user-centred student information literacy instruction. *The Journal of Academic Librarianship, 32*(1), 79–85.

Chapter 2

Six Frames for Informed Learning

Opening Narrative

Steve and Jane meet to discuss their experience of building information practices into their students' learning experiences. They discover that they have both met with surprisingly mixed reactions from their colleagues. At a school meeting, someone came down very heavily on the idea of using portfolios for assessment, while other staff were very interested. Another colleague was a little puzzled at what Steve was trying to do. He also believed that information capabilities were very important, but surely students should have those skills before they arrive? Or perhaps those matters could be left to the librarians and study skills advisers?

Jane is finding that a few of her students are complaining that she isn't teaching them anything. They are not used to learning content through process. Access to the resources Jane has made available as a starting point, the regular support of the reference librarian, and access to each others' papers for the conference do not seem substantial enough. Steve has learned that the art librarian is able to work with him in his teaching and has begun by pointing his students to a wide range of interesting resources.

*Steve and Jane are discovering that many people have an interest in informed learning, but that they all come to it with different perspectives, using different sets of lenses that are informed by their own teaching values and understandings of information and information use. Steve and Jane search the Internet and discover the **Six Frames for Informed Learning**. They begin to see where their own values lie and to understand the views of others. They see that they were both primarily working through the Learning to Learn frame and that some others around them, including their students, are working through the Content and Competency frames. They wonder if it might help their students if they worked a little more through the Personal Relevance frame.*

Informed learning draws from what we know about variation in the experience of learning and teaching. In this chapter, I explore how the idea of informed learning may be approached differently in curriculum depending on the conceptions of learning, information, and other dimensions adopted by those involved. Six Frames for Informed Learning identifies several dimensions that may vary depending on the personal experiences and view of those involved, including approach to assessment, information use, teaching, learning, information, and content.

Informed Learning Draws From Our Understanding of the Experience of Learning and Teaching

Since the early 1980s, a unique picture of the experience of learning and teaching has emerged from a constantly evolving research base. Many of the research studies involved were conducted initially in Sweden, the United Kingdom, and Australia. Interest in that work has since spread to the United States, Pacific Islands, and other places in Europe and Asia, particularly Hong Kong. Much of the research has been done by, or in collaboration with, teachers engaged in classroom practice. The primary outcome of this work has been the emergence of the view that learning involves coming to appreciate the different ways in which it is possible to see or experience the object of learning (Marton & Booth, 1997). These differences are usually referred to as the variation in the ways of seeing or experiencing particular concepts, professional problems or forms of professional practice.

In this view, the primary task of the teacher is to understand students' ways of seeing, whatever it is they are learning. As educators, we then need to help students encounter different ways of seeing the phenomenon we are teaching so that they will understand those differences and have a sense of which lenses are more appropriate for them to use. With some things we teach, some lenses may appear to be better than others; in other cases, the different ways of seeing are simply different.

This view of teaching and learning has come to influence how we see overarching educational concerns such as competence, graduate capabilities, and transfer. Like learning, competence may be thought of as seeing the world in particular ways or as experiencing practice in particular ways (Dall'Alba & Sandberg, 1996). Similarly, we can help students respond appropriately to new situations, thus transferring their learning, by helping them to see the similarities and differences between situations (Marton, 2006).

Simon Barrie (2006) applies this approach to the graduate capability agenda, discovering that some of us see that agenda as separable from discipline teaching. Sometimes, we adopt the lens of seeing the graduate capability agenda as being about skills, most of which are prerequisite to higher-order learning in the discipline. At other times, we use the lens that sees the agenda as inseparable from discipline or professional learning, an integral element of evolving expertise. When we see the graduate capability agenda as inseparable from discipline or professional learning, we successfully merge or fuse the learning of such capabilities with content learning.

What Are the Six Frames for Informed Learning?

The Six Frames are lenses through which our experience of learning and teaching for informed learning might be viewed. The lenses that each of us chooses will reflect our own interests and values and those of our disciplines. A balanced curriculum across a whole program would ideally include aspects of all the frames. In practice, there is usually an emphasis on those frames that concur with the requirements of institutional policies and other accrediting bodies.

The frames were developed as a conceptual tool to help colleagues interested in informed learning to reflect on and analyze the varying implicit or explicit theoretical influences on their contexts. The frames were developed by bringing together thinking about variation in approach to teaching, learning, and information use with thinking about approaches to curriculum design and the idea of viewing problems through identifiable frames (see, for example, Bolman & Deal, 1997). Toohey (1999), Ramsden (2003), Prosser and Trigwell (1999), or Bruce (1997) would serve as useful texts for further exploration of ideas underlying these frames.

What Do the Six Frames for Informed Learning Look Like?

Each of the Six Frames is associated with particular views of information literacy, information, curriculum focus, learning and teaching, content, and assessment. Some elements of each frame apply to both the discipline content being learned and to the information use component where these are taught together. In describing each frame, I provide an example to illustrate practice implemented primarily through that frame.

The Content Frame for Informed Learning

Table 2.1 The Content frame for informed learning	
View of information literacy	Information literacy is knowledge about the world of information.
View of information	Information exists apart from the user; it can be transmitted.
View of learning and teaching	Teacher is an expert who transmits knowledge. Learning is a change in how much is known.
Curriculum focus	What should learners know about the subject and about information literacy?
View of content	What needs to be known has primacy. All relevant content must be covered.
View of assessment	Assessment is objective. It measures how much has been learned. Students are ranked via exams.

Using the Content Frame for Learning Design

Imagine that you are teaching students about the ethics of your discipline and that you want them to learn how to engage with the information environment effectively as they learn about the ethics.

If you adopt the Content frame, you would provide lectures dealing with key content in ethics, and you would probably invite a librarian to provide some lectures or tutorials about relevant information sources and ask students to do some searching of their own in the area. You would ask students to consider what they have learned as they seek information, but you are unlikely to emphasize that process through assessment or discussion.

You may use quizzes to give students feedback on their progress. You would assess by examining their knowledge about ethics and test what they have learned about important information tools.

A sample curriculum objective might be: You will know about ethics in your discipline and the resources available to you for learning ethics.

When looking through the Content frame (Table 2.1) we usually adopt a "knowledge about the discipline" orientation. Our focus is on what students should know about their subject and about the world of information. Our assessment would typically quantify how much has been learned. In relation to informed learning, a typical example might be providing lectures or online information about useful information tools and techniques, for example, online databases or reference management systems. Learning might be assessed through examination of recall. Similarly, we may expect students to receive and be examined on knowledge about how information is organized or made available in their discipline. We expect that discipline experts will do the discipline teaching, and librarians may teach aspects of the information curriculum.

The Competency Frame for Informed Learning

Table 2.2 The Competency frame for informed learning	
View of information literacy	Information literacy is a set of competencies or skills.
View of information	Information contributes to the performance of the relevant capability.
View of learning and teaching	Teachers analyze tasks into knowledge and skills; learners become competent by following predetermined pathways.
Curriculum focus	What should learners be able to do?
View of content	Content is derived from observation of skilful practitioners.
View of assessment	Assessment determines what level of skill has been achieved.

When using the Competency frame (Table 2.2) we usually adopt a behavioral or performance orientation. We ask what students should be able to do, and at what level of competence? We may prescribe a set of instructional modules for students to follow to attain the required competencies. We assess students by attempting to determine what level of skill has been achieved. A typical example might be the design of sequenced instruction to teach the use of an electronic tool, supplemented by testing to determine the level of skill that has been attained by the learner at specified points in the learning process. We may wish to ensure that students are competent Internet searchers and evaluators of Web-based content. This goal in this frame could be achieved by arranging for self-paced instructional packages to be made available, packages that allow for the validation of having completed particular levels of instruction.

Using the Competency Frame for Learning Design

Imagine again that you are teaching students about the ethics of your discipline and that you want them to learn how to engage with the information environment effectively as they learn about the ethics.

If you adopt the Competency frame, you may choose to have students work with a series of ethical cases, determining the key aspects of each case and making decisions about what action it may or may not be appropriate for a stakeholder to take, thus gradually building ethical competence. You would direct students towards self-paced, self-testing instructional packages to help them learn about the information processes and resources that they will need to continue to learn about professional ethics. You would probably set an assignment to encourage them to use information to extend their understanding of ethical issues and debates; you are likely to focus attention on the skills they would use in this process.

You might provide feedback on their skill development through the self-paced packages or by setting the assignment in two or three parts. You would assess their competence in dealing with ethical cases and in the information environment through testing the level of skill they have attained in ethics and in using the information environment.

A sample curriculum objective might be: You will be able to make ethical decisions in complex professional contexts and will be able to use the resources available to you to continue learning about professional ethics.

The Learning to Learn Frame for Informed Learning
When using the Learning to Learn frame (Table 2.3), we usually adopt a constructivist orientation. We ask what it means to think like an information-empowered professional, for example, an architect, engineer, journalist, or landscape designer. We are also interested in what will help students construct knowledge appropriately and develop learning processes that foster the development of professional thinking patterns. Our assessment seeks to determine how information processes have informed students' learning or their approach to the problem at hand.

Table 2.3 The Learning to Learn frame for informed learning

View of information literacy	Information literacy is a way of learning.
View of information	Information is subjective; it is internalized and constructed by learners.
View of learning and teaching	Teachers facilitate collaborative learning; learners develop conceptual structure and ways of thinking and reasoning.
Curriculum focus	What does it mean to think like an informed learner in the professional environment?
View of content	Content is chosen for helping students to master important concepts and for fostering reflective practice.
View of assessment	Complex, contextual problems are proposed. Self or peer assessment is encouraged.

Discipline experts and information professionals, especially librarians, may work separately or together in setting a real-life problem in which the need to access, evaluate, and use information from a range of sources is central and appropriately supported. For example, business students or engineers may work on a case study that requires analysis, interpretation, and the identification of apparent problems that need solving or issues that need resolution.

Using the Learning to Learn Frame for Learning Design

Imagine again that you are teaching students about the ethics of your discipline and that you want them to learn how to engage with the information environment effectively as they learn about the ethics.

If you adopt the Learning to Learn frame, you may again choose to have students work with a series of ethical cases. You would have students conduct their own research. You would encourage them to work with a range of types of information, people, blogs, research articles, and their own experience to help them understand the issues embedded in the cases. You would also ask them to think regularly about what they are learning and how they are using information to learn.

You may choose to set an assignment to encourage them to use information to extend their understanding of ethical issues and debates. You would also ask them to reflect on their learning and information use as they engage with that assignment. In this frame, you may choose to work with a librarian to help students think through the resources they are accessing and what these resources mean. The librarian would also work with you and your students to enhance awareness of the information environment.

You may work with the librarian to provide feedback in class or online. You would assess the quality of students' interpretation of ethical issues and also their reflections on how they have gone about learning and using information.

A sample curriculum objective might be: You will use a range of resources to engage with ethical cases and will reflect on how your use of information has influenced your engagement with the cases.

The Personal Relevance Frame for Informed Learning

Table 2.4 The Personal Relevance frame for informed learning	
View of information literacy	Information literacy is learned in context and is different for different people or groups.
View of information	Valuable information is information that is useful to the learner.
View of learning and teaching	The teacher focuses on helping learners find motivation. Learning is about finding personal relevance and meaning.
Curriculum focus	What good is information literacy to me?
View of content	Problems, cases, and scenarios are selected to reveal relevance and meaning.
View of assessment	Assessment is typically portfolio-based; learners self-assess.

When looking through the Personal Relevance frame (Table 2.4), we usually adopt an experiential orientation. We need students to develop a sense of what creative and reflective information use can do for them. We may be interested in the kinds of experiences that are required to enable students to engage with the subject matter. Assessment in this frame is typically portfolio-based, and the students self-assess. We could ask students to participate in a topical project that requires engagement with relevant information services and providers; students would also be asked to reflect on their experience and what they learned about both the subject and information use in that context. Personal relevance could range from researching the job market, to collecting stories from members of the community, to creating exemplars of work undertaken for communication to a broader community.

Using the Personal Relevance Frame for Learning Design

Imagine again that you are teaching students about ethics in your discipline and that you want them to learn how to engage with information effectively as they learn about the ethics.

If you adopt the Personal Relevance frame, you may do much that is familiar from previous frames. You could ask students to work with a series of ethical cases. You would ask them to conduct their own research, working with a broad range of types of information, people, blogs, research articles, and their own experience to help them understand the issues embedded in the cases. You would also ask them to think regularly about what they are learning and how they are using information to learn.

In this frame, you would ask students to (a) establish their own learning objectives, and (b) determine how they would demonstrate accomplishment of those objectives. You would also ask them to consider how what they are learning and the information processes they are using to learn may impact their personal lives now or in the future.

For feedback, you may ask students to self-assess and seek the comments of their peers, as well as gaining input from the teacher or tutor. For assessment, you may ask them to submit a portfolio of work demonstrating and reflecting on how they have met their chosen objectives.

A sample curriculum objective might be: You will determine your own learning objectives in the area of professional ethics. You will reflect on how professional ethics and the information processes you are using may influence your personal lives and professional careers.

The Social Impact Frame for Informed Learning

Table 2.5 The Social Impact frame for informed learning	
View of information literacy	Information literacy issues are important to society.
View of information	Information is viewed within social contexts.
View of learning and teaching	The teacher's role is to challenge the status quo. Learning is about adopting perspectives that will encourage social change.
Curriculum focus	How does information literacy impact society?
View of content	Content reveals how information literacy can inform widespread or important social issues or problems.
View of assessment	Assessment is designed to encourage experience of the impact of information literacy.

When we look through the Social Impact frame (Table 2.5), we usually adopt a social reform orientation. Our interest turns to how informed learning impacts society and how it may help communities deal with significant problems. It is also important for students to understand the importance of valuing information and information-use practices of different kinds and from different cultures. A typical example might involve focusing students' attention on various issues and values associated with problems surrounding the digital divide and proposing tasks related to policy, technology, or training designed to assist in bridging that divide. Students may, for example, be assessed on their understanding of how information use and appropriate technologies could impact the social problem. They could be asked to communicate their findings to different groups of people—children in primary schools, indigenous women, or professionals in the field.

Using the Social Impact Frame for Learning Design

Imagine again that you teaching a group of students about ethics in your discipline; you want them to learn how to engage with information effectively as they learn about the ethics.

If you adopt the Social Impact frame, you may again establish a similar context, for example, choosing to have students work with a series of ethical cases. You would ask students to do their own research and to work with different types of information such as people, blogs, research articles, and their own experience to help them understand the issues embedded in the cases.

In this frame, you would also ask students to consider how their information-use processes are helping them to see or not see the social implications embedded in their cases. You may ask students to consider the potential impact on, for example, individuals, organizations, cultural and other groups, or society at large of actions taken or decisions made and to consider what information may have been taken into account in making those decisions. You may also ask them to consider how relevant policies may need to be developed to protect groups or areas from negative impact.

For assessment, you may ask students to communicate what they have learned to a group of stakeholders. Feedback might be sought from industry or community stakeholders.

A sample curriculum objective might be: You will consider how different professional decisions in a particular case may impact society.

The Relational Frame for Informed Learning

Table 2.6 The Relational frame for informed learning

View of information literacy	Information literacy is a complex of different ways of interacting with information.
View of information	Information may be experienced as objective, subjective, or transformational.
View of learning and teaching	Teachers bring about particular ways of seeing specific phenomena. Learning is coming to see the world differently.
Curriculum focus	The focus is on bringing about awareness of the critical ways of seeing or experiencing.
View of content	Examples or strategies are selected to help students to discover new ways of seeing. Critical phenomena for learning must be identified.
View of assessment	Assessment is designed to reveal ways of seeing or experiencing the phenomenon.

When we look through the Relational frame (Table 2.6), we are concerned with the ways in which our students experience informed learning or related phenomena. We focus on understanding students' experiences and then designing learning to focus or expand that experience. We design experiences to help our students use a wider range of lenses when working with the phenomena in question. Our assessment is developed to identify which lenses students have learned to use when engaged with informed learning or other relevant phenomena. Reflection is one strategy to encourage students to discern more complex forms of the phenomenon.

Using the Relational Frame for Learning Design

Imagine again that you are teaching students about ethics in your discipline and that you want them to learn how to engage with information effectively as they learn about the ethics.

If you adopt the Relational frame, you may again choose to have students work with a series of ethical cases. You would ask to students to research the issues, working with a broad range of types of information, people, blogs, research articles, and their own experience to help them understand the issues embedded in the cases.

In this frame, you would ask them to articulate their own views about the cases and help them to see the different views emerging among peers. You may also ask them to identify significant differences in the ways in which particular matters are dealt with in the cases. And you may ask them to identify what they consider to be relevant information and how that information informs their view of the case, then help them to distinguish the differences that emerge around that.

Students would receive feedback from their interaction with you and their peers around the above matters. You may choose to assess students' ability to identify and make use of the different lenses that may be brought to an ethical issue.

Sample curriculum objectives might be: You will consider the decisions you might make in a specific case from a range of professional perspectives. You will identify differences between your own and others' views of professional ethics. You will explore the different types of information that inform the different views of professional ethics.

Particularly interesting is the status of the Relational frame as one through which the Content, Competency, Learning to Learn, Personal Relevance, and Social Impact frames are mediated, or brought together. When using the Relational frame, we see informed learning as a complex of different ways of using information to learn within which an experiential approach is taken to:

- knowledge about the world of information (Content frame);
- competencies or skills (Competency frame);
- learning through engagement with information (Learning to Learn frame);
- contextual and situated social practices (Personal Relevance frame);
- power relationships in society and social responsibility (Social Impact frame).

When we use the Relational frame, we are interested in both content (phenomena) and the lenses through which that content is seen or experienced. In the example above, we would notice students dealing with professional ethics as content knowledge, as a competency where they know what to do as ethical professionals, as an area that requires continuous learning, as an area that may impact their own lives, and as an area that has social consequences.

Principles Associated With the Six Frames for Informed Learning

- Informed learning is experienced differently by stakeholders (teachers, students, administrators) across the university involved in policy making, curriculum design and approval, and design of learning tasks.
- Educators and learners in the same context may experience informed learning differently at the point of implementation. Whether learning is occurring virtually or in a face-to-face situation, those involved will always see what they are doing differently.
- Different stakeholders in the same context will have frames that they prefer to adopt through which they view informed learning. These frames may or may not match those of their colleagues, the curriculum they are working with, or the organizational framework.
- The frames are complementary and need to work together, although one might be dominant and others in the background. We need to know what content we want people to learn through the appropriate processes.

Using the Six Frames to Bring About Informed Learning

How can we use the Six Frames for Informed Learning?

- First, to shed light on the values and views of colleagues, students, and others.
- Second, to make possible innovation.

As members of the learning community, we are all challenged by (a) diverse ways of experiencing learning and (b) diverse ways of experiencing informed learning. When we have difficulty conveying our ideas or difficulty understanding the viewpoints of another, it is likely to be because we are seeing the world through different frames. Understanding those alternative views helps us to at least stand in the shoes of others and then to find ways of working together to bring our complementary interests and strengths to existing or developing programs.

The greatest value of the frames lies in their power to challenge each of us to identify our primary frame or frames and to inquire into how our professional practice might develop if we were willing to adopt a different frame or a wider range of frames.

Key Questions Arising From This Chapter—What Can We as Educators Do to Take This Agenda Further?

If your students are engaged in any information practices, or if your curriculum emphasizes information literacy in any way, then you have opened the door to informed learning. Use the questions below to help you consider further informed learning in your context.

Informed Learning and Your Philosophy of Teaching

- What are your views of learning, teaching, competence, graduate capabilities, or lifelong learning?
- What are the views of your students and colleagues?
- How might this diversity be influencing your teaching/ learning environment?
- Which frame or frames resonate with your experience?
- What relationships can you see between your views of teaching and learning and your preferred frame or frames for informed learning?

Informed Learning and Your Students
- Which frames for informed learning might your students be adopting?
- How could you find out if there are conflicting frames operating in your classroom and what they might be?
- How could you encourage the adoption of frames that you prefer your students to be working through?
- Identify something that your students need to learn, and describe what their learning experience might look like through each of the different frames.

Informed Learning and Your Curriculum Practice
- Which frame or frames for informed learning are now dominating your practice?
- How might your practice, course, unit, lectures, or assignments change if you adopted alternative frames?
- Describe your present practice and proposed future practice.

Informed Learning in Your Field
- Which frames for informed learning best reflect curriculum directions in the pedagogy of your field or discipline?
- How could the other frames contribute?

Note: This chapter adapts the Six Frames for Information Literacy Education (Bruce, Edwards, & Lupton, 2006) to the informed learning context. The reworking of the concept around informed learning reinforces my position that informed learning is a fundamental purpose and direction for information literacy education.

References
Barrie, S. C. (2006). Understanding what we mean by the generic attributes of graduates. *Higher Education, 51,* 215–241.

Bolman, L., & Deal, T. (1997). *Reframing organisations: Artistry choice and leadership* (2nd ed.). San Francisco: Jossey-Bass.

Bruce, C. S. (1997). *The seven faces of information literacy.* Blackwood, South Australia: Auslib Press.

Bruce, C., Edwards, S., & Lupton, M. (2006). Six frames for information literacy education: Exploring the challenges of applying theory to practice. *ITAL-*

ICS Special Issue Information Literacy—The Challenges of Implementation, 5(1) http://www.ics.heacademy.ac.uk/italics/vol5iss1.htm

Dall'Alba, G., & Sandberg, J. (1996). Educating for competence in professional practice. *Instructional Science, 24,* 411–437.

Marton, F. (2006). Sameness and difference in transfer. *The Journal of the Learning Sciences, 15,* 499–535.

Marton, F., & Booth, S. (1997). *Learning and awareness.* Mahwah, NJ: Erlbaum.

Prosser, M., & Trigwell, K. (1999). *Understanding learning and teaching: The experience in higher education.* Buckingham, UK: Society for Research into Higher Education and Open University Press.

Ramsden, P. (2003). *Learning to teach in higher education.* London: Routledge, Falmer.

Toohey, S. (1999). *Designing courses for higher education.* Buckingham, UK: Society for Research into Higher Education and Open University Press.

Chapter 3

Seven Faces of Informed Learning

Opening Narrative

*Steve and Jane decide that they need to help their students see more clearly what they are learning by engaging in the information practices that have been selected for them. Steve and Jane are seeking a model built from an investigation of professional practice and are pointed towards the **Seven Faces of Informed Learning.** They are told that the Seven Faces were constructed on the basis of conversations with academics from a wide range of disciplines about their professional practice. Steve and Jane decide to explore the model with their students and to discuss with students the experiences of informed learning to which they are being exposed.*

Steve and Jane are pleased to find that in this model, information use is interwoven with technology use; they are also interested that in this model, successful information interaction is treated as being a social rather than an individual practice.

Some of Steve's students are very anxious about some forms of technology, and he realizes that he needs to reassure them that they are not expected to become technology gurus. Rather, they are expected to accept the need to be interdependent, to give help where they can and to seek it when they need to. Jane realizes that she needs to encourage her students to look beyond technology to forms of information outside the Internet and to take an interest in the social consequences of what they do with information and their own knowledge.

Steve and Jane also discover that each of the ways of experiencing informed learning is associated with a particular way of focusing attention on the information interaction. Designing a variety of learning experiences that encourage the different foci is one way to enhance the informed learning experience.

Informed learning draws from our understanding of how we use information as we learn. In this chapter, I explore the Seven Faces of Informed Learning as a transdisciplinary model of learning through engagement with information. The Seven Faces of Informed Learning model underpins most information practices in academic and professional settings. It is a relational model, developed through investigating people's experiences, and it contributes to the Relational frame for informed learning described in chapter 2. Selected examples show how the faces may be applied to designing learning tasks and invigorating curriculum.

Informed Learning Draws From Our Understanding of the Experience of Using Information to Learn

In chapter 2, I looked at the Six Frames for Informed Learning, a curriculum framework that encompasses a number of approaches that may be adopted when teaching for informed learning. In this chapter, I look at the experience of informed learning from the perspective of academics and other professionals. This is the phenomenon, the experience of informed learning, that we want to become a part of students' experience.

What does it mean to help students become insightful, wise, and capable as they engage with knowledge and information on their present and future learning journeys? This is one of the challenges arising from a focus on informed learning. As our information environment continues to grow and diversify and the quality of information becomes more difficult to discern, being able to work effectively with information becomes increasingly important for learning, professional practice, and everyday life. This chapter outlines a picture of informed learning that has been developed through investigating the information-use experiences of a range of professionals and discipline experts. The Seven Faces of Informed Learning described here reveal aspects of the experience of information use that we may wish to develop in students. The faces are ways of using information while learning that are applicable across disciplines.

What Are the Seven Faces of Informed Learning?

The Seven Faces of Informed Learning reveal different ways in which information use is experienced as we go about learning in our professional, academic, and everyday lives.

The Seven Faces were developed on the basis of research participants' responses to a small number of questions focusing their attention on

Figure 3.1 The Seven Faces of Informed Learning	
WISDOM	**EXTENSION**
KNOWLEDGE CONSTRUCTION	
PROCESS	**CONTROL**
SOURCES	
INFORMATION AWARENESS	

information use, for example: *How do you use information at work and in everyday life?* All the participants worked as educators at universities in different fields, including law, engineering, nursing, and education.

The faces are designed to reveal variation between the experiences. This attention to variation allows us to understand critical differences in our ways of experiencing informed learning. The faces also suggest learning outcomes based on whole experiences and real-life practice. In order to reveal the critical differences between the Seven Faces, the structure of each experience is described in terms of:

- What we are concentrating on, or are *focused* on, in that experience. This aspect appears as the central circle in the graphical depictions of each face (figures 3.2–3.8).
- What is in the background, which we are not concentrating on but are still aware of. This aspect appears as the middle circle.
- What is closer to the margin of our experience, sometimes called the perceptual boundary, the point beyond which we do not see. This aspect appears as the outer circle.

Using the Seven Faces to Inform Learning

It is the structure of each experience that shows us important aspects of how to introduce students to informed learning. For example, in the first face, information technologies and their use are in focus. In the second face, information sources are in focus. The sixth face emphasizes creativity and innovation, and the seventh face ethical information practice. Reading the details of the experience will highlight nuances in the experience that need to be reinforced. For example, in the first face, the social nature of using technology to learn and the importance of being empowered are vital. In the second face, the value of working with a librarian to gain the benefit of his or her professional expertise is key. Each of the descriptions of the Seven Faces below also includes a brief example of how the face could be used in learning design. The examples are intended as suggestions only of how the faces could be applied.

Another important aspect of the structure of the informed learning experience is the shifting place in awareness of information technology and information use across the Seven Faces. In the first face, information technology is the point of focus; in the seventh face, it is at the outer edge of awareness. In the first face, information use is in the margins of the experience, and in the seventh face, information use is the point of focus.

In addition to the structure, the Seven Faces of Informed Learning show us that information itself may also be experienced differently. These ways of experiencing information are summarized towards the end of this chapter. An extended description of the Seven Faces is available in *The Seven Faces of Information Literacy* (Bruce, 1997).

What Do the Seven Faces of Informed Learning Look Like?

Each of the Seven Faces is described below. The descriptions include graphical depictions of the critical components of each face. I have also included ideas about how students could be helped to access each face and examples showing how the faces may be used to influence learning design.

The First Face: Informed Learning Is Experienced as Using Technology to Communicate and Keep Abreast of Developments in the Field
In this face of informed learning, information and communication technologies take central place. These would include mobile and wireless technologies, as well as other computers that give access to information and communication networks and provide the necessary software for reading and communicating. The primary purpose of technology in this experience is to bring information into awareness, or to enable communication.

Figure 3.2 The First Face: The Information Awareness and Communication Experience

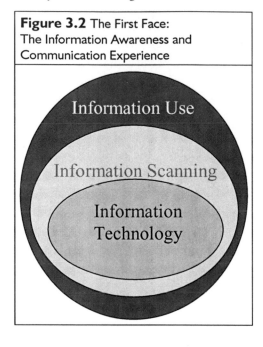

When we experience informed learning this way, we see using information technology as essential for information awareness, and we see that this is achievable within a supportive community of users. This experience has come out of the lives of high-achieving professionals, including many academics, who recognize that their own personal competence is interdependent with the larger fabric. One academic said, "... it is hard in isolation. You need people to help. Then everyone becomes expert in slightly different aspects and is available to help and teach the others."

This experience is about community, and it challenges our individualistic, rational ways of approaching the world. It reminds us that technology has power for good and that using technology for information awareness and communication is empowering. Such use of technology empowers cultures and subcultures, giving voice to women, children, and others. New, socially oriented Web technologies (Web 2.0), such as wikis, blogs, and Second Life, become a powerful force in facilitating this experience.

In this first experience, where individual capabilities are meaningless against the capabilities of society at large, the need to accept that using information well is necessarily a social experience challenges the very bases of our educational systems, where the need to monitor, assess, and certify the performance of individuals is pervasive.

In order to help students access this experience, we must help them put on the appropriate lens when engaged with informed learning. In this case, we need to direct their attention toward using technology to communicate and scanning for information. In doing so, it is also important to emphasize the social nature of the experience. When we ask them to use new and innovative technologies, or indeed any technologies, we need to ensure that they are well-supported and that they don't feel alone in their efforts.

Using the First Face for Learning Design

Imagine that you are teaching a first-year class on professional practice in your field. You have already created teams of students who will be working on a collaborative project.

In order to focus students' attention on using technology for communication, you invite them to use e-mail, blogs, and other strategies to communicate and stay informed about progress of individual members of the team. To enable feedback and assessment, you ask individual students to

- report on how their communication strategies supported their project;
- provide examples of times when they offered support to, or were supported by, team members or others in their use of the technology.

To focus students on using technology for information awareness, you invite them to use conference pages, blogs, Google searching, bulletin boards or chat rooms, professional Web sites or newsletters, push technologies, and shared spaces to learn about an aspect of their discipline and report on it. To enable feedback and assessment, you ask the team to report on

- the user-friendliness of the different technologies;
- what they have learned from each;
- how these resources may assist them as students or as professionals.

An appropriate learning outcome might be: Students will support each other as they use contemporary technologies to develop an awareness of current developments in the field.

The Second Face: Informed Learning Is Experienced as Sourcing Information to Meet a Learning Need

In this face of informed learning, information sources take central place. When we experience informed learning this way, we are focused on the different types of sources available to us, the need to be aware of those sources, and effective ways of accessing them.

We need resources for our work and for our personal lives. We are aware of the need to work with and through technology to gain access to some of the resources we need. Such resources include other people and their expertise, as well as resources appearing in text

Figure 3.3 The Second Face: The Sourcing Information Experience

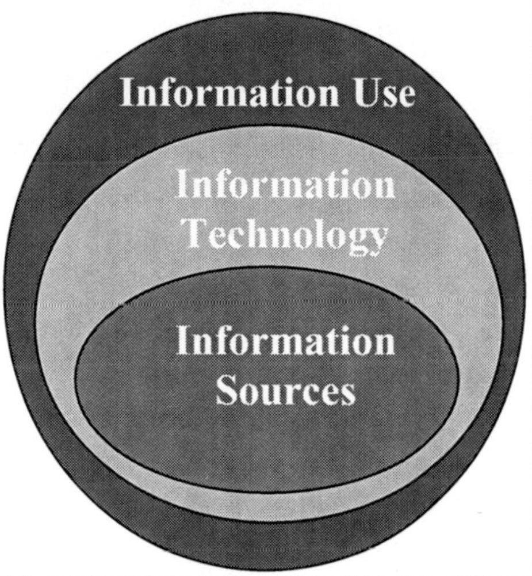

or other media. The purposes for which we will use the resources are within our perceptual boundaries and influence the sources we are interested in. When experiencing informed learning this way, people may say that they know what they want, if not how to get it, and that they are not afraid to ask to find an answer—they will ask people who do know.

In this experience also, we are aware of the need to rely not only on our own knowledge and abilities, but on information professionals, especially librarians, as mediators able to assist us to maintain our information environment and provide training. We value, and sometimes take for granted, the need for personal skills, but wish also to be able to rely on information professionals when we need to. While we are aware of information technology, it is not our primary concern, as access to sources may not always involve working with ICTs.

When helping students access this experience, we need to direct their attention towards a range of information sources. In doing so, it is also important to give them experience of working with information professionals and gaining the benefits of professional expertise. We also need to consider the forms of information that are important in our profession or discipline and decide which of these we wish to introduce to our students (see chapter 5).

Using the Second Face for Learning Design
Imagine that you are teaching a first-year class on professional practice in your field.

In order to focus students' attention on sourcing information, you give them an assignment requiring research. You may ask them to

- first, find their own materials and resources;
- then locate materials based on a librarian's recommendations;
- finally, reflect on the relative value of the two sets of outcomes for their purposes.

Provide feedback on and assess students' search outcomes and their reflections for variety and relevance.

An appropriate learning outcome might be: Students will work independently and with the assistance of a librarian to access different types of information sources as they learn about a particular topic.

The Third Face: Informed Learning Is Experienced as Engaging in Information Processes to Learn
When we experience informed learning this way, we are focused on the processes we choose to engage with when we are using information. These processes are usually linked to the need to solve problems or make decisions.

When choosing a path, we do not confine ourselves to the established patterns recommended by information professionals and others. We are more likely to treat the information process as a creative art, one that requires the identification and adoption of personal heuristics to be successful. When we experience informed learning this way, we are aware of information technology,

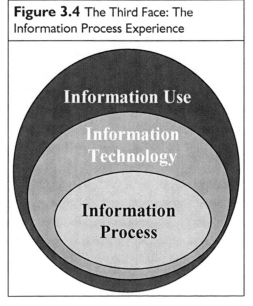

Figure 3.4 The Third Face: The Information Process Experience

Information Use

Information Technology

Information Process

but it is not our primary concern, as we may choose to use or not use ICTs according to our own preferences.

When giving students access to this experience, we need to help them use a different lens. They need to become aware of the processes they use and with which they are comfortable and also to consider alternatives that they may choose to add to their repertoire.

Using the Third Face for Learning Design

Imagine that you are teaching a first-year class on professional practice in your field.

You have decided to introduce them to the Third Face of Informed Learning and now need to focus students' attention on their information processes. You design an assignment requiring research and ask students to

- describe their usual information-use processes;
- try a different process recommended by the teaching staff or peers;
- consider what was new in what they did, how they would prefer to operate in future, and why.

Alternatively, you could ask student to

- describe their information processes and the outcomes;
- comment on why they used the processes they chose;
- comment on what might have been the result of using different processes.

Provide feedback by asking students to share and comment on each other's emerging processes in class.

Assess their reflections for critical thinking about the implications of their actions and possible alternatives.

An appropriate learning outcome might be: Students will explore their information processes and articulate their preferred approaches.

The Fourth Face: Informed Learning Is Experienced as Making Connections Between Information and Learning Needs

In this experience of informed learning, information control takes central place. When we engage in informed learning this way, the intended purposes for which we want information influence our experience of information control. The projects, problems, activities, and people in our daily life are important and serve as hooks to which we link information that we encounter.

Information control begins when we *recognize information encountered as potentially relevant to a project or purpose.* We make connections between the information, people, current tasks, or possible future activities. Once that *connection is made, we manage information by locating it somewhere* using our technology of choice.

Figure 3.5 The Fourth Face: The Information Control Experience

Information Use

Information Technology

Information Control

One possible way of locating or placing the information is by storing its "place" in our brain. When we do this, we simply know where to go for what we need. We have the capacity to recall what we encountered previously and where to locate what we need in a personal collection or in the wider information environment. The second way in which we might locate information is through the use of a paper-based filing system, collating relevant material in a single place, whether this be a file, a box, or a more sophisticated manual system. The third possibility is the use of electronic files, spreadsheets, and databases. Using a combination of strategies is also possible. Comments such as the following show that different individuals have different preferences: "Well ... somehow he has the sort of brain that he can use as his filing cabinet which I can't do. I use my filing cabinet as my brain."

Information technology is present in people's awareness; the purposes for which information is being used inform the manner in which information is controlled.

When we help students access this experience, we direct their attention towards information control and the technologies that assist this. It is important to help them make connections between the information they are using and the projects they are working on.

Using the Fourth Face for Learning Design

Imagine again that you are teaching a first-year subject on professional practice in your discipline. You have already created an assignment that requires students to engage with a range of resources, and you now wish to direct students towards the Fourth Face.

In order to focus students' attention on making links to various parts of their project, you ask them to create a concept map of the different aspects of their research. You also ask them to use the key aspects they have identified as one or more of the following:

- labels for physical files for storing information they gather
- a subdirectory structure for electronic resources they find
- categories for Internet bookmarking
- categories in a database
- headings in their paper or report

Provide feedback by asking students to share and discuss their concept maps with peers and tutors. Assess by asking students to write a short reflection on how their information control strategies helped or hindered them and what they would do differently in future.

An appropriate learning outcome might be: Students will control information.

The Fifth Face: Informed Learning Is Experienced as Building a Knowledge Base in a New Area of Interest

When we experience informed learning this way, critical analysis is our key strategy for engaging with information, and coming to know is central. We consider knowledge, not as objective, but rather as adopting a personal stance on the topic at hand based on a critical, analytical reading of relevant resources.

Critical analysis may be interpreted as identifying gaps in knowledge, recognizing conflicting schools of thought, and assessing the reliability of research. It is also about researching your own thoughts, a process of clarification. The following comment explains how this might work: "What's happening in the process is that I'm able to say, '…he says that about it because of the way he's approaching the subject or because of his previous experience or his expertise in the particular area of the field. She's approaching it from here. Where do I stand in relation to those two? I prefer that way of looking at it.'"

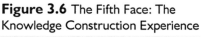
Figure 3.6 The Fifth Face: The Knowledge Construction Experience

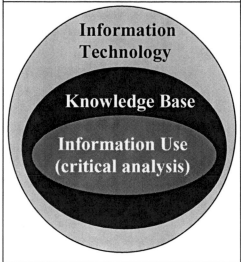

In this experience, information use has a vital role to play in developing an understanding of previously unfamiliar territory. Our emphasis is on learning about something that has come to be of interest, and learning is usually about understanding different views on that area of interest. Information in this experience may come from participating in Internet discussions, reading documents, listening to the radio, talking to people in a public place, or using databases. Interacting with people, in person or virtually, is a very significant part of this experience, helping us to build knowledge of the field and see it in particular ways. Critical thinking is therefore a vital tool in the exploration of new territory. We are aware of information technology when experiencing informed learning in this way, but it needs to be unobtrusive in the thinking process.

When we help students to access informed learning this way, it is important to help them focus on the different perspectives they encounter as they engage with texts, people, or other resources to learn about their area of interest.

Using the Fifth Face for Learning Design

Imagine again that you are teaching first-year students a professional practice subject in your field. You want them to understand that they are empowered to learn about areas of interest previously unfamiliar to them.

In order to focus students' attention on critical thinking, you dedicate one class session to an activity where students identify existing and emerging areas of interest that they would like to learn more about. You then require individuals or small groups to select an area of particular interest to them and each week to:

- identify community, professional, or research resources in their area of interest;
- discuss what they have learned from each resource;
- discuss the different perspectives and assumptions or biases that are implicit or explicit in each resource;
- identify the perspectives, assumptions, or biases that appeal most to them and discuss the reasons for this appeal.

For feedback and assessment, individuals or teams could be asked to write or present a brief summary of what they have learned about the content area and the process on two successive occasions: early in the teaching period and towards the end.

An appropriate learning outcome might be: Students will develop a knowledge base in a previously unfamiliar area.

The Sixth Face: Informed Learning Is Experienced as Extending Knowledge

In this experience of informed learning, intuition, as a key strategy for engaging with information, is central. When we experience informed learning this way, we work with an enhanced knowledge base, a knowledge base that incorporates our own background, insights, and experience. We draw upon a combination of our knowledge base acquired through wide and deep reading and the knowledge we have acquired through personal experience; we then use creative insight or intuition to evolve new knowledge or approaches to tasks or novel solutions.

When we describe such an experience of information use, we may talk about the act of creating something new as a mysterious process: "I think there's a creative relationship really... You can stuff yourself

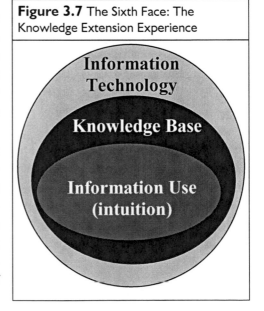

Figure 3.7 The Sixth Face: The Knowledge Extension Experience

Information Technology

Knowledge Base

Information Use (intuition)

full of information and only be capable of regurgitating that, but actually to synthesize and relate it to other things, come up with something new... I find that just happens spontaneously, you make connections... I still find it a rather mysterious process."

As information is used creatively, new knowledge is produced. Creativity and intuition make new information possible. Inspiration allows us to see connections between previously unrelated information.

When we help students access informed learning this way, it is important to encourage them to draw on their personal knowledge, experience, and insights.

Using the Sixth Face for Learning Design

Imagine again that you are teaching first-year students a professional practice subject in your field.

In order to focus students' attention on their intuitive capacity, ask them to create something new, whether this is a new solution to an existing problem, the identification of new problems or hypotheses, or an interpretation of an artistic work.

Encourage students to think about and share with each other what knowledge they drew upon and how their intuitive or creative capacities influenced their work.

For feedback or assessment, ask students to present a portfolio documenting their creative process. This may take the form of multiple iterations of their work and a reflection focused on the knowledge they have drawn upon, as well as how their own creativity influenced the work.

An appropriate learning outcome might be: Students will build upon their own knowledge and perspectives to gain new insights.

The Seventh Face: Informed Learning Is Experienced as Making Wise Use of Information for the Benefit of Others

In this experience of informed learning, adherence to personal and professional values is central. Being an informed learner is about our whole person and our interrelationship with others. It is about bringing to bear personal qualities, combining values and ethics with acquired knowledge in making decisions, solving problems, or counseling.

Wise use of information occurs in a range of contexts, including exercising judgment, making decisions, and doing research. It involves recognizing that information and information technologies could be used appropriately or inappropriately, for subjection or empowerment, to exploit or to benefit. It also involves recognizing that we can choose to use them for the benefit of others: colleagues, clients, family, friends, or society at large. Informed learners have an awareness of their own beliefs, values, and attitudes and of how these frame their practice.

When we use information this way, information access, and consequently technologies, are on the periphery. One user comments, "Accessing information doesn't really come into it...information is not simply utilitarian...people have values and those values are brought to the using of information."

When we help students access informed learning this way, it is important to help them become aware of their values, attitudes, and beliefs and to help them accept their social responsibilities.

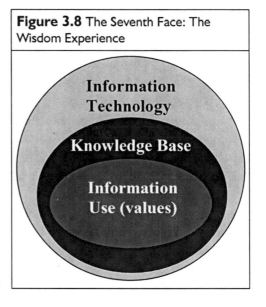

Figure 3.8 The Seventh Face: The Wisdom Experience

Information Technology

Knowledge Base

Information Use (values)

Using the Seventh Face for Learning Design

Imagine again that you are teaching first-year students a professional practice subject in your field. For this face, you would need to incorporate a client or social context into the learning design.

In order to focus students' attention on their values and how those values influence their use of information, you might, for example, ask them to document the information they choose to use or not use, what they choose to communicate to others or not, and why. In identifying solutions to problems, ask students for alternative solutions based on the situations of relevant stakeholders.

For feedback or assessment, ask students to make explicit how their beliefs and values have influenced their decisions.

An appropriate learning outcome might be: Students will use information with awareness of their capacity to benefit others.

The Changing Experience of Information Across the Categories

As we use information differently, information appears or presents itself to us differently. In examining the experience of informed learning, learners and information are the two key elements that stand in relation to one another. In that relation, we look at information from a particular perspective, and information presents itself to us differently. We engage with and transform information; information engages with and transforms us. When we consider information as it is experienced and recognize the transforming character of information, traditional separations between data, information, and knowledge become fused; there is no need to conceptually differentiate them or represent them as part of a hierarchy.

What is information? Information is anything we experience as informing. What we may experience as information appears to have few limits. In chapter 5, I will show how what we experience as information also differs across contexts.

In the different ways of experiencing informed learning, information may present itself as:

• *Transformational.* Information appears this way in the sixth and seventh faces. We experience information as transformational in character: either able to be transformed, or able to transform us as we engage with it. When we experience information this way, it is not part of the external environment, but rather an integral part of ourselves. When information appears as transformational, it is inextricably entwined with beliefs, values, and attitudes. It is this fabric that makes possible the use of information for the benefit of others, as seen in the seventh face.

• *Subjective.* Information is most likely to appear this way in the fifth face. We experience information as subjective, a focus of reflection. As a consequence, ways of interpreting the information form part of our knowledge base. Here too, information experienced this way is an intrinsic part of who we are.

• *Objective and contextualized.* Information is most likely to appear this way in the third and fourth faces. We experience information as objective, and the information appears to us from within the context or purpose for which it will be used. The information presents itself as part of an external environment, and knowledge is required to access it. Personal strategies, such as information processes or control, are required for us to bring the information within our sphere of influence.

- *Objective and decontextualized.* Information is most likely to appear this way in the first and second faces. We experience information as objective, part of an external environment, and knowledge about that environment is required to access it. In the first face, this knowledge is primarily about technology. In the second face, it is knowledge of sources.

Principles Arising From the Seven Faces of Informed Learning

What the principles arise from the Seven Faces of Informed Learning? Each of the five principles listed below comes from looking across the Seven Faces for important themes:

- There are several different ways in which we may experience the character of information and using information to learn.
- Our preferences and unique ways of working with information should be respected and encouraged.
- The relative importance of information technology varies in each experience.
- Information literacy, including information technology use, is a social phenomenon more than an individual one.
- There is a strong relationship between information literacy and learning.

In bringing together our different experiences of using information to learn, the relational model of informed learning promotes a holistic learning approach that balances

- ICT confidence and skills, as we encourage students to participate in the online community and navigate and access the online environment;
- communication skills, as we encourage students to exchange information and share new insights;
- analytical and evaluative capability, as we encourage students to develop and conduct information strategies and assess information resources;

- critical and creative approaches, as we encourage students to make sense of information and construct new knowledge;
- social responsibility, as we encourage students to use information ethically and wisely (adapted from Hughes, Bruce & Edwards 2007, p. 62).

Using the Seven Faces to Bring About Informed Learning

The Seven Faces of Informed Learning suggest broad learning outcomes and describe the kinds of experience students need to engage with to achieve these outcomes. Often students are already engaging with activities that require them to use information in order to learn; they may need to become aware of what they are doing or learn more effective ways of going about it.

As educators we can use the Seven Faces of Informed Learning to help build curriculum. We need to

- diagnose the existing range of learners' information literacy experiences;
- deepen the experiences with which they are familiar;
- usher them into previously unfamiliar experiences.

We also need to design learning experiences that relate to relevant faces and help students experience for themselves different facets of information use. The examples that appear with the Seven Faces in this chapter are intended to suggest possible directions that could be taken. One concern that is likely to arise as such design processes are undertaken is that of ensuring that students do not get tired of being asked to report on aspects of their informed learning experience. Central to this concern are issues around course or program design. If programs are being coordinated as a whole, then it is important to identify a range of strategies for assessing or evaluating students' achievement; it is also important to determine key components of the program in which to focus attention on the information-use experience.

We need to explore, then, in our own disciplines, how academic curricula can be designed to encourage students to experience the different faces of informed learning; perhaps modifying the Seven Faces to better suit the needs of the discipline. How can physical scientists, health scientists, computer scientists, engineers, artists, historians,

musicians, mathematicians, and others design curriculum that requires
students to
- use information technology for information awareness and
  communication;
- come to know a range of bibliographic, human, and
  organizational information sources;
- develop personal heuristics for the application of information
  processes;
- control information through establishing, mapping, or
  formalizing relevant connections;
- adopt a critical approach to knowledge construction;
- exercise their intuitive capacities to gain new insights or
  understandings;
- draw upon personal values or ethics when using information.

Suggestions for Learning Design

Prompts we could use to help students focus on some of the different
experiences of informed learning include:
- Describe how you use information technology as you go
  about learning.
- Describe how you gather information as you go about
  learning or working on a project.
- Describe any processes or information strategies you may
  have developed that help you learn when you were working
  on a project.
- Describe how you recognize and manage information that
  you see as being valuable.
- Describe how the way you use information has helped you
  develop your understanding of your field, topic, subject, or
  discipline.

Contributed by Doug Colbeck, University of Tasmania, Australia.
These questions are adapted slightly from those used to interview
students in a recent research project, 2007.

Curriculum that takes the notion of informed learning seriously
would embrace the full range of experiences across an entire program

of study such as an undergraduate degree. Course or program coordinators could use the Seven Faces for evaluation and program monitoring. Evaluation or monitoring exercises could compare curricula against the experiences of informed learning presented here, or a modified version adapted for your discipline, to establish representation and identify gaps.

Informed Learning Brings the Different Ways of Using Information to Learn to Students' Attention

We need to help our students to become comfortable with the different experiences of informed learning and to learn to recognize when they are, or when they could be, engaging in the relevant experience. The two examples below illustrate different aspects of how we could use the Seven Faces model with groups or individuals.

In this first example, the Seven Faces model was used in a single unit of study to broaden students' experience of informed learning. The students were learning about information use in a business school. These students were asked several times during a course of study to reflect on their personal experience of information use, with the intention of making them think about their learning in this area. One of the tasks in which students were engaged was the evaluation of a Web site from multiple perspectives—seen as a marketing tool, seen as an information source, and seen from the point of view of usability. As students were encouraged to think about their use of information and learning, they made a discernible shift from information technology and information sources approaches towards information evaluation and management approaches. The class was taught using a Relational frame, encouraging students to broaden their information literacy experience (Johnston &Webber, 2003).

In the second example, we see how the Seven Faces model may be used to diagnose learning difficulties so that we can help students adopt an appropriate way of understanding their experience. Susie Andretta (2008, p. 6) describes a student going through the motions of creating a concept map. She set down ideas and drew lines between related ideas as a precursor to writing. The student later reflected that the strategy failed for her because she was not able to see that she was engaged in a process of information organization (Face 4) and knowledge construction (Face

5). She went through the motions of concept mapping because she was asked to and shown how to, but she was not given any understanding of the purposes for which she was engaged in the activity. Andretta reports the student as saying, "To me it was just putting down a map of ideas, but I wasn't seeing how the connecting [would enable me] to write a structured essay...It's about organising knowledge."

If we return to the Fourth Face, we will see that, in people's experience, the purposes for which information or knowledge is organized is a critical element of the experience. Clearly, if no connection is made between the purpose and the organization process, then the latter is meaningless. It is also possible that the teacher in the case may have restricted herself to using the Competency frame in her curricular approach to informed learning: providing a skill without attention to the Learning to Learn or Personal Relevance frames.

Key Questions Arising From This Chapter—What Can We as Educators Do to Take This Agenda Further?

The Seven Faces of Informed Learning give us a set of experiences that we can adapt or use as desirable learning outcomes for our students. Some possible questions to pursue arising from this chapter include:

Informed Learning and Your Philosophy of Teaching
- Which faces of informed learning reflect your own experience?
- How do your teaching and your expectations of students reflect your own experiences?

Informed Learning and Your Students
- How can you discover which experiences of informed learning are being adopted by your students?
- What can you do to make students aware of the lenses they are adopting?
- What can you do to expand the repertoire of the lenses students are adopting?

Informed Learning and Your Curriculum Practice
- Are there any lenses you would prefer your students to adopt more regularly?

- How can you help students to do so?
- What criteria could you use to provide feedback or help assess students' use of information for learning?

Informed Learning in Your Field
- How do your colleagues experience informed learning?
- Which faces most closely reflect the experience of informed learning in your discipline?
- How could you revise the Seven Faces to be more relevant to your discipline or professional practice?

Note: This chapter draws from *The Seven Faces of Information Literacy* (Bruce, 1997). The reworking of the material around informed learning is intended to reinforce my position that information literacy is fundamentally about using information to learn.

References

Andretta, S. (2008, in press). Facilitating Information Literacy Education (FILE). In A. Brine (Ed.), *Handbook of library training practice and development (Vol. 3)*. Aldershot, England: Gower Publishing.

Bruce, C. S. (1997). *The seven faces of information literacy*. Blackwood, South Australia: Auslib Press.

Hughes, H., Bruce, C., & Edwards, S. (2007). Models for reflection and learning: A culturally inclusive response to the information literacy imbalance. In S. Andretta (Ed.), *Change and challenge: Information literacy for the 21st century* (pp. 59–85). Blackwood, South Australia: Auslib Press.

Johnston, B., & Webber, S. (2003). Information literacy in higher education: A review and case study. *Studies in Higher Education, 28*, 335–352.

Chapter 4

Students' Experiences of Informed Learning

Opening Narrative

What other work has been done associated with informed learning that may be of assistance to Jane and Steve? As they progress in their teaching, they realize how important it is to understand how their students perceive or experience information tasks the students are engaged in and to help the students find new ways of experiencing these tasks. They also discover that the Relational approach to informed learning suggests many possible directions for curriculum design and evaluation at both undergraduate and graduate levels.

In an advanced class, Steve creates a case around new graduates setting up their own studio and marketing themselves as artists. He invites the art librarian to work with him and the students as they engage in the case. He starts by talking with her and the students about the Seven Faces of Informed Learning and which of those faces they should concentrate on as they work with the case.

Jane discovers that the Seven Faces research has been implemented in the undergraduate setting and that several other investigations have been conducted into different ways in which aspects of information use are experienced. Again, most of the ways of experiencing proposed are accompanied by ways of focusing that provide clues about how to direct students' attention.

Many of the examples that Steve and Jane find provide insights into others' experience, which they can share with their own students. Steve and Jane are beginning to discover a wider community of academics from different fields, all of whom have been working for some time in their area of emerging interest.

Informed learning draws from our understanding of students' experiences. Helping students become better at using information in order to learn begins with understanding their experience of informed learning. In this chapter, I examine information use from the student perspective: how they use information as they go about learning. I then explore students' experiences of some information practices that influence learning, such as Internet searching, essay writing, and assignment writing, and that are of relevance across disciplines and cohorts. I also explore strategies for encouraging reflection that brings about learning.

Informed Learning Draws From Our Understanding of Students' Experiences of Information Literacy

In the last chapter, I looked at informed learning from the perspective of academics and professionals and showed how their experiences of using information form an important part of the overall picture. In this chapter, I look at students' experiences of informed learning, including their experience of various information practices that form a part of their academic journey.

Several investigations have been conducted into students' experiences of information literacy and academic information practices. Most of this work has been conducted in Australia, Europe, and the United States. In this chapter, I examine contemporary understandings that help develop the picture of informed learning. Here, under the umbrella of informed learning, I draw together a range of studies into learners' experiences of information literacy and their experience of a variety of information practices. In all these examples, students are using information to learn. Most of the research findings presented are relevant across a range of cohorts and disciplines.

Having an understanding of students' experiences provides us with further guidance for curriculum design and evaluation. In curriculum design, we need to establish which experiences are critical for our learners and to create learning opportunities that make it possible for students to engage with those experiences. We are then in a position to develop reflective strategies to enhance students' awareness of different aspects of informed learning. In curriculum evaluation, we need to make professional judgments about whether or not our curriculum is providing the breadth of experience necessary and make changes to improve our students' learning experiences.

As I showed in chapter 3, insights into students' focus as they engage in particular ways of experiencing are a significant aid in designing learning to bring about those experiences. Most of the research outcomes reported here include attention to students' focus as they experience the phenomenon under investigation.

Later in the chapter, I open up the question of the relationship between students' ways of interpreting the content they are learning and their interaction with the information environment.

Helping Students Learn Is About Understanding Their Experience of Informed Learning.

In the previous chapter, I explored informed learning from the perspective of professionals and academics across a range of disciplines. I identified the different experiences of informed learning as potential learning outcomes for learners in higher education. In order to best help students learn, it is also helpful to have an understanding of their experience. All the studies in this chapter describe students' experience of informed learning. Each attends to different aspects of that experience. In the three studies immediately following, students' experiences with information literacy are explored; then another group of studies explores students' experience of learning through specific information practices: essay writing, assignment writing, and Internet searching. The studies of information literacy reveal the ways in which students experience the relationship between information literacy and learning, their more general experience of information use, and their experience of learning information literacy. Many of students' experiences are closely related to the Seven Faces of Informed Learning (chapter 3), a feature that I have highlighted wherever it is relevant.

Helping Students Become Informed Learners Is About Understanding Their Experience of the Relationship Between Information Literacy and Learning

Much of the research reported throughout this chapter highlights the very close relationship between information literacy and learning. The experienced nature of that relationship was the direct subject of an investigation conducted by Mandy Lupton (2008). Lupton explores students' experience of the relationship between these two phenomena in the domains of music and accounting (see below). As a result, she proposes that, across disparate disciplines, the relationship between information literacy and learning can be experienced in three different ways:

• *As sequential.* In this experience, students see the relationship between information literacy and learning as linear. They see themselves as first acquiring information and then, at a later time, learning from that information. Acquiring information may be acquiring a technique, and using information may be applying that technique; for example, being trained in the use of software and then using that software. This sequential experience is achieved through the application of information techniques, such as academic writing, referencing, or database or Internet searching. The linear relationship experienced by students is depicted in figure 4.1.

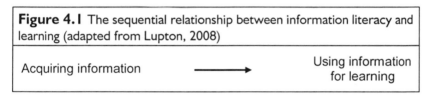

Figure 4.1 The sequential relationship between information literacy and learning (adapted from Lupton, 2008)

Acquiring information   ⟶   Using information for learning

• *As cyclic.* In this experience, students see the relationship between information literacy and learning as cyclic. They see themselves as first acquiring, then using information, then acquiring further information to enable them to continue the learning process. They see themselves as going through the sequential processes in a recursive way, as part of a journey of discovery. They get information, learn from it, get more information, learn more, get more, learn more, and so on. The cyclic relationship experienced by students is depicted in Figure 4.2.

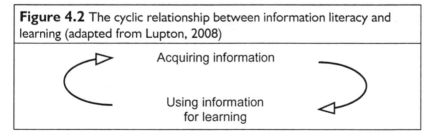

Figure 4.2 The cyclic relationship between information literacy and learning (adapted from Lupton, 2008)

Acquiring information

Using information for learning

• *As simultaneous.* In this experience, students see information literacy and learning as inseparable. They experience information use and learning as concurrent, inseparable activities. They do not distinguish between acquiring and using information; these stand in a simultaneous relationship, as they do with learning. The two happen at the same time, as two sides of a single coin; for these students, information is internal, a part of themselves, as well as textual, digital, or aesthetic. Information is not sought; it is interacted with as they use it to learn. The simultaneous relationship experienced by students is depicted in Figure 4.3.

Figure 4.3 The simultaneous relationship between information literacy and learning (adapted from Lupton, 2008)

Using information: learning

Mandy Lupton also concludes that we cannot learn without using information in its various forms, not only textual information, but information generated by processes, by using our senses, and by acknowledging emotions and ideas.

What does this mean for us as educators helping students learn? It means that, in accordance with the principles of informed learning, we need to present information use and learning to our students as inseparable activities. If we are presenting students with apparently technical information practices, such as retrieval and organization, we need to ensure that we are encouraging them to maintain a focus on what they are learning about their field or project along the way. We also need to talk with them about using their learning tasks, and the information practices intrinsic to them, as learning opportunities.

Suggestions for Learning Design

Mandy Lupton notes that we may be doing our students a disservice when we design curriculum that encourages a sequential approach to information use and learning. She suggest that teaching students about techniques that will only later be applied in a learning task encourages a sequential experience; using problem-based or enquiry learning strategies and requiring regular phases of reflection encourages a cyclic approach; requiring students to maintain blogs or reflective journals that document their ongoing reflection on information use and learning encourages a simultaneous approach (Lupton, 2008).

Music Students' Experience of Informed Learning

Music students were one of the groups with which Mandy Lupton worked when investigating the experienced relationship between information literacy and learning. Her research reveals the value of understanding students' experiences of informed learning in the context of specific disciplines. How do music students experience informed learning? Lupton (2008) proposes that, in that discipline, the experience of using information to learn may be experienced as craft, process, or art. These students identified information as sound, music theory, and composers' techniques, among others (see table 5.1). They identified using information as involving copying composers, experimenting, trial and error, learning to listen, communicating, and creating sound. The process and art experiences show similarities with the Process and Knowledge Extension faces of informed learning (chapter 3).

- *In the craft experience*, students experience the relationship as "the craft of creating a composition through applying techniques." They focus on acquiring and applying techniques as both forms of learning and forms of using information. Specifically, they see learning as acquiring skills, and they see information use as using software to create and manipulate sound. The two elements, acquiring and applying, are experienced sequentially. Students see themselves as first acquiring the technique, then applying it.

- *In the process experience*, students experience the relationship as "creating a composition through a cyclic process of discovery." They focus on composing sound, which for them constitutes information, and engage in an iterative, or cyclic, process that is a journey of discovery. They see learning as a self-directed process of developing a craft, and information use is seen as listening, experimenting, and allowing oneself to be taught by the process. The elements in the process are experienced cyclically.

- *In the art experience*, the relationship is experienced as "the art of creating a composition through expressing oneself." Here, students focus on self-expression; for them, learning the craft and engaging in art occur simultaneously. They see learning as personal development, and art as involving self-expression, creating and communicating one's identity and ideas. Information use is seen as drawing on one's inner resources, paying homage to experienced composers, and building personal identity and self-expression. Information use and learning are experienced simultaneously.

Suggestions for Learning Design

Mandy Lupton recommends that, in courses where creativity is an important goal, learning should be designed to allow students to simultaneously learn the craft and engage in art. We can draw students' attention to the distinction between how information is used in *craft* and *art*.

Tax Law Students' Experiences of Informed Learning

When working with tax law students, Lupton (2008) identifies that these students' experience of the relationship between information literacy and learning differs from the experience of music students. The tax law students whom she interviews experience the relationship as applying academic techniques, discovering the big picture, or understanding the tax law system. The discovery and understanding experiences appear to be closely related to the Knowledge Construction and Wisdom faces of informed learning (see chapter 3). These students identify information as techniques, such as mind mapping or research, texts, such as legislation or case law, and viewpoints or clients' perspectives.

- *When applying academic techniques,* students experience the relationship as "a sequential process of applying academic techniques to complete the assignment." In this experience, students focus on applying techniques. Learning and using information are seen as being about the development and application of techniques, such as legal research, academic writing, and referencing. They see learning tax law as being about learning the techniques. Using information is seen as citing references, writing for the layperson, and conveying limited information to the client. Acquiring and then applying the techniques are experienced sequentially.

- *When discovering the big picture,* the relationship is experienced as "a cyclic process of discovering the big picture on a tax law topic." Students focus on the topic they are researching and the many viewpoints from which that topic may be approached. They see learning tax law as learning about the topic, and information use as selecting or developing a personal perspective, seeing links and relationships, or using evidence to support the argument. Students see information use and learning as occurring cyclically.

• *When understanding the tax law,* the relationship is experienced as "a cyclic process of understanding the tax law system for professional practice, for one's personal situation and for social impact." Students focus on the tax law system and their professional practice. They interpret learning tax law as coming to understand the system and seeing the implications for oneself, one's clients, and society. They interpret information use as forming opinions in order to advise clients, advising and giving clients options, staying aware of tax law developments, and addressing their own personal situations. Students see information use and learning as inseparable.

The tax law students interviewed by Mandy Lupton were doing the same learning tasks and were being taught by the same teacher. Yet clearly what they gained from the learning experience differed because of the differences in what they were attending to in their experience. In the case of music students, there were two groups, two assignments, and two teachers. Yet in these groups also, students' experiences of going about learning as they interacted with information differed. From research like this, we can see that we can empower our students, deepening their learning, by drawing their attention to appropriate approaches to both learning and information use.

Suggestions for Learning Design

Mandy Lupton recommends that learning should be designed to help learners see the personal, professional, or social impact of their information use and learning. We can draw students' attention to how information is used in the more complex learning experiences.

Helping Students Become Informed Learners Is About Understanding Their Experience of Information Literacy

Some cross-disciplinary insights into undergraduate students' experience of informed learning are also available from the results of studies conducted at the California Polytechnic State University at San Luis Obispo. Clarence Maybee (2006) shows that across a student cohort, more than one approach to information use is likely to be already present. His findings confirm that undergraduate students' views are aligned with the Seven Faces of Informed Learning (Sources, Process, and Knowledge Construction). As may be expected, they are not as rich as those of more experienced academics, which I described in chapter 3. Maybee interviewed students from different majors, year levels, and genders and identified three key ways of experiencing information use among undergraduate learners:

• *Information use is seen as finding information located in sources.* In this way of seeing, students orient themselves towards information location. They focus on information sources, and information use is seen as a secondary, separate activity occurring at a later time. Students talking about using information this way emphasize their knowledge of different sources, how the sources are organized, and the various tools available for locating information, such as keyword searching of databases. Students also place some emphasis on evaluating, on the basis of its source, the quality or "credibility" of information retrieved. Maybee provides an example of a female computer science student who identifies published, edited books as being more trustworthy than Internet sites.

• *Information use is seen as initiating a process.* In this way of seeing, students orient themselves towards initiating and operational zing a process. They focus on their process. Information use occurs during the process, with information location becoming an iterative activity as the purpose for which it is being used evolves. Students talking about information this way place some emphasis on the relevance and the quality of what they find. Maybee provides an example of a male business administration student who prefers pertinent, unbiased, objective information to large quantities of information.

• *Information use is seen as building a personal knowledge base for various purposes.* In this way of seeing, students are oriented towards themselves as "knowers." They focus on the purposes for which information is used, for example, making decisions, solving problems, forming personal perspectives, sharing information, or constructing new knowledge. The knowledge base itself takes a background place. Students talking about information this way emphasize the need to understand the viewpoint of the author or producer of the resources they are using. They are keen to apply their knowledge to new areas.

Maybee (2006) also notes that, in the sources and process views, students consider information to be objective and separate from themselves; while in the knowledge base experience, they see information as subjective, something that is now a part of themselves.

How do undergraduate women experience information literacy? Maybee (2007) shows that the experiences of this group closely resemble those described in the Seven Faces (see chapter 3). When undergraduate women focus on information technology, the need to access relevant sources via technology is in the background. When they focus on processes or sources, then information use is in the background. When they are focused on information use, their knowledge base supports that use. Maybee's description of undergraduate women's experiences also indicates that at some times information must be obtained before it can be used; while at other times using information is experienced as building a knowledge base and, for these students, information is an integral part of who they are. These findings are similar to Lupton's descriptions of students experiencing the relationship between information use and learning as sometimes sequential and sometimes simultaneous.

The outcomes of such investigations provide us with a platform on which to build and the opportunity of introducing the idea of informed learning to student groups using descriptions such as these, with which they are likely to identify. Part of our responsibility is to ensure that learners understand and develop the information use experiences with which they are already familiar. We then have the challenge of introducing them, over their program of study, to the full range of experiences so that they can discern and use all Seven Faces of Informed Learning

Suggestions for Learning Design

Clarence Maybee reminds us that some students will look for information for an assignment with "little regard for the learning experience inherent in the assignment." Later they will use this material to do the required work. Other students will, for the same assignment, seek a deeper understanding of the area as they interact with information, connecting their information and learning goals. It is the latter approach that we should promote to help students become informed learners (Maybee, 2007).

(see chapter 3). We also have the challenge of ensuring that students link their information practices with their learning, which is the primary direction of informed learning.

Helping Students Become Informed Learners Is About Understanding Their Experience of Learning Information Literacy

How do students experience learning information literacy? And why does it matter? Using information to learn is something that must itself be learned. As we have seen through Clarence Maybee's and Mandy Lupton's studies, we can expect that university students will have experience of learning through information use. We can also expect to be able to influence their experience, once we understand it, by encouraging them to see through alternative lenses, adopt different foci, and therefore engage with information in different ways.

Rae Anne Locke (2007) has conducted a study that shows us that, when students describe their experience of learning information literacy, their descriptions also closely reflect the Seven Faces of Informed Learning. As experiences of informed learning and students' experiences of learning information literacy are not dissimilar, we can use the research outcomes with confidence in learning design.

Locke explains that students experience learning information literacy as:

- *Learning to find information.* When focused on finding information, students want to develop skills and are keen to learn by doing, using trial and error, and gaining help from more skilled teachers and peers along the way. This experience is associated with fluctuating feelings of frustration and excitement; other emotions include confusion, anxiety, comfort, and familiarity. It is closely aligned with the Accessing Sources face of informed learning.

- *Developing a process for using information.* When focused on processes for information use, students want to develop more effective and efficient approaches to their context and are willing to learn by doing, using trial and error, exchanging ideas, or collaborating with peers along the way. This experience is also associated with excitement when students find a process that works, frustration when they do not. It is closely aligned with the Process face of informed learning.

- *Learning to use information to create and construct.* When focused on their product, usually an artifact or assignment, students want to learn their subject content and to learn to use information to further that learning and to help build their product. They are keen to discuss their learning with others. This experience is associated with excitement when things are working, frustration when they are not. It is closely aligned with the Knowledge Construction and Knowledge Extension faces of informed learning.

- *Building a personal knowledge base in a subject area.* When focused on learning content, students want to learn their discipline, to reflect, to internalize, and to develop their own knowledge. They use others to help them develop their understanding. This experience is associated with anticipation, pleasure, and love of learning. It is also closely aligned with the Knowledge Construction face of informed learning.

- *Advancing disciplinary knowledge.* When focused on advancing knowledge, students want to create new knowledge through research and investigation. They work with a self-selected group of key people who can help them work through their ideas. This experience is associated with frustration, risk taking, and growing confidence as a researcher. It is closely aligned with the Knowledge Extension experience of informed learning.

- *Learning to use information to grow as a person and to contribute to others.* When focused on their role in the community, students want to keep walking their learning journey and to contribute to those around them. They achieve their learning and contribution through relationship

Suggestions for Learning Design

All the studies I have explored so far in chapters 3 and 4 show that there are a range of ways of experiencing informed learning. Often, as teachers interested in information literacy, we focus our students' attention on information sources and finding information because learning to find information is important and difficult. When we do this, we are in danger of drawing their attention away from other aspects of learning to use information. We need to resist the temptation to teach information sources from a sequential perspective. We can help avoid this danger by sharing other students' experiences and by asking our own students to think about how their own experience reflects the broader spectrum.

building. This experience is associated with enthusiasm, energy, and generosity. It is closely aligned with the Wisdom experience of informed learning (Locke, 2007).

Researching Assignments, Essays, and Internet Searching: Educating Informed Learners Is About Understanding Students' Experience of Academic Information Practices

In addition to general investigations into students' experience of information literacy and information use, we also have insights into the relationships between students' experiences of information use and their learning approaches and outcomes. Research into this area suggests that, in most learning situations, superficial approaches to information use are likely to correlate with superficial learning outcomes. I have selected the following examples to show how learners engaged in typical information practices display differences in their learning about content (in the first example) and their approach to learning (in the second example).

Researching Assignments

A study conducted in Sweden by Louise Limberg (2000) shows how students researching an assignment come to understand their area of study differently. As a result of particular ways of experiencing information seeking and use, they come to understand content in particular ways. She identifies a connection between students' information-seeking and information-use processes and the way in which they come to understand the consequences of European Union (EU) membership for Sweden. Limberg suggests that differences in students' understanding of their topic influenced how they approached searching for and using information. At the same time, differences in their approach to information searching influenced their understanding of their topic. She finds that

- Students who experienced information seeking and use as "fact finding" could not assess for themselves the consequences of EU membership for Sweden. These students tried to find the right answers to the question, and consequently could not find answers.
- Students who experienced information seeking and use as "balancing information in order to choose the right side" saw the EU as being mainly about economic cooperation and were able to identify advantages

and disadvantages associated with this view. These students, as they interacted with information, were attempting to adopt a neutral position in their assessment of debate and found that increasingly difficult.

• Students who experienced information seeking and use as scrutinizing and analyzing information in order to understand the topic area saw the EU as a power bloc and membership as a matter of political or ethical commitment.

Insights From the Six Frames and Seven Faces of Informed Learning

Can the Six Frames and Seven Faces models give us any insights into the student experiences Limberg describes? Given the nature of the task that students were set, we might say that the teacher was adopting a Social Impact frame (chapter 2) in her learning design.

While we do not have concrete evidence about the informed learning lenses that students were adopting, it appears that it is only in the third experience that students were adopting a Knowledge Construction or Wisdom lens (chapter 3).

Researching Essays

While Limberg has shown how learning outcomes are associated with information use, Lupton (2004) shows how students' approaches to learning are associated with their information-use experiences. Mandy Lupton provides insights into first-year undergraduate learners' experiences of information use while researching essays. Her students were developing an essay around the topic "Managing resources is about managing people, not resources." She writes that students' experiences indicate " ... an interrelationship between the essay task, information and learning" (2004, p. 54). These three things are closely linked for students whom she describes as

• *Seeking evidence.* In this experience, learners focus on the essay as a course requirement, seek information in order to answer questions posed by the teacher, and do not see themselves as learning or developing a knowledge base in the area.

• *Developing an argument.* In this experience, learners focus on the essay as a topic for learning, seek information in response to questions they are asking themselves, and see themselves as developing a knowledge base in the area.

- *Concerned with social responsibility.* In this experience, learners focus on the essay as an opportunity to communicate and learn about the discipline and the field; see information as a vehicle for making connections between the topic, field, or discipline and other disciplines; and see themselves as applying their learning to the area of investigation and consequently contributing to social change.

Mandy Lupton concludes that students seeking evidence appear to be adopting a surface or atomistic approach to learning. Students developing an argument appear to be adopting a deep or holistic approach to learning. Students seeing learning as a social responsibility appear to be adopting a transformative approach to learning, where influencing society is an important outcome.

Insights From the Six Frames and Seven Faces of Informed Learning

Can the Six Frames and Seven Faces models give us any insights into the student experiences Lupton describes? Using the Six Frames to look at Mandy Lupton's results suggests that the teacher's curriculum approach may have resembled the Social Impact frame for informed learning.

Students seeking evidence may have benefited from discussions about informed learning as knowledge construction. Students developing an argument are likely to be already adopting a knowledge base approach to informed learning and may have benefited from a deeper understanding of that lens. Students seeing learning as a social responsibility may also have benefited from understanding their perspective through becoming familiar with the idea of informed learning as using information wisely.

Internet Searching

Not infrequently, the products of our students' inferior Internet searching come to our attention. Clearly, Internet searching is an important information practice in today's academic and professional environment, and students need to learn to adopt a critical and reflective approach to information use in the online world. Often, inadequate assignment submissions result from students' relying on inappropriate information because they have a poor understanding of the Web-based information environment they are using. Investigating undergraduates' experiences of searching the Internet, Sylvia Edwards (2006) identifies that students can be helped to improve their search capabilities and understanding of Web resources by focusing their attention differently and engaging them in reflection and planning. Edwards uses metaphors to capture the character of students' different Internet searching experiences:

- *Students experience information searching as looking for a needle in a haystack.* These students are likely to give up searching as a result of frustration. They focus on understanding their topic but do not have any discernment of the structure of the Web environment. They are not planning or reflecting on the information they find and have no appreciation of the differences in the quality of the resources they encounter. Students might describe their searching as largely involving trial and error.

- *Students experience information searching as finding a way through a maze.* These students persist with their searching, but have not yet acquired the reflective skills to achieve high-quality results. They are focused on both their topic and the process of searching, but do not yet understand the complexities of the Web environment or the nuances in the quality of information it may deliver. Students might describe their searching as somewhat like being on a quest or navigating a maze.

- *Students experience information searching as filtering.* These students are likely to be successful in their search for useful resources. They focus on the structure of the Web environment and how its search capabilities can help them, but are not well engaged in planning or reflection, the evaluative and recursive processes necessary for the highest quality outcomes. Students might describe their searches as needing to be refined or filtered.

- *Students experience information searching as panning for gold.* These students are likely to find high-quality resources as a result of planned and reflective searching and a capacity to evaluate critically.

Suggestions for Learning Design

Using Sylvia Edwards' research, I would construct a learning task such as the following: Learners will keep a diary in which they reflect on which lenses for Internet searching they might be using and what they are learning about their discipline area as they work with each lens.

They focus on the structure of the Web environment, their topic area, and the character of the resource base they are encountering. Students might describe the need for finding primary or quality sources, the sources that everyone else points towards.

The close linkages between information use and learning suggest that, as educators, we need to attend closely to students' experience of academic practices and content learning, as well as their experiences of informed learning. Limberg shows how information use is closely entwined with learning outcomes; Lupton and Edwards show us that considering essay writing and Internet searching as both academic and information practices is likely to benefit informed learning.

Other Academic or Information Practices Could Be the Subject of Classroom Investigation—The Case of Portfolio Development

Perhaps the information practice you ask students to use is not considered in this chapter. Often, when teaching, we ask students to use an information practice that has not yet been researched. If that is the case, consider conducting your own classroom-based investigation, as I did when my students were creating portfolios to showcase their learning. Implementing portfolio development requires use of the Personal Relevance frame for informed learning and requires students to be able to use the Information Control and Wisdom faces. Portfolio development requires students to identify and draw together a wide variety of information, such as reflections and artifacts that may take different forms.

Using a short questionnaire I found that my students were seeing their portfolio as:

- *A form of assessment.* Students seeing their portfolio this way adopted an assessment-oriented approach and were focused on completing the assessment task. Students adopting this approach claimed to be looking at the task required, going through the lists of what is suggested, and compiling the required evidence. They may have neglected to develop useful and interesting material because they were focusing on the academic task, rather than using it as a vehicle for employment preparation or professional development.

- *A tool in the job-search process.* Students seeing their portfolio this way adopted an employment-oriented approach. Students adopting this approach focused on the value of the portfolio in preparing themselves for interviews and employment. The portfolio, for them, is seen as a tool in the job-search process. In this and subsequent approaches, the assessment task becomes secondary to personal interests.

- *A reflective tool.* Students seeing their portfolio this way adopted a reflective approach. Students adopting this approach focused on their own development and understanding. The portfolio, for them, becomes primarily a tool for facilitating reflection.
- *A tool for job search and reflection.* Students seeing their portfolio this way adopted a combination of the pragmatic and reflective approaches. Students adopting this approach seem to successfully focus on both preparation for employment and personal development simultaneously.

There appear to be three distinct levels at which students can approach the task. The first and most simple level is captured in the first approach: students are interested only in completing the academic task as set. At the second level, students are bringing one of two personal interests to the experience, focusing on either the job-search aspect or the reflective component. At the third level, students are combining both of these foci effectively. These levels may be set out as follows:

- Level one: assessment approach
- Level two: employment or reflective approach
- Level three: combination of employment and reflective approaches

I was able to use these insights to raise the question of how to help students see the approach they were adopting and the alternative possibilities (Bruce & Middleton, 1999). I was able to explore how to direct class thinking and activity towards both the reflective and employment approaches.

Learners' Views of What They Are Learning Influence the Extent of Their Information Environment

Is it possible that learners' view of their discipline, or the content of what they are learning, might influence their engagement with the world of information? Or perhaps that learners' engagement with the information environment may influence their view of their discipline? The outcomes of a number of investigations into students' learning and information use suggest this may be the case. An analysis of the information universe inhabited by these students suggests that those with more complex views of their discipline inhabit a wider information universe.

Limberg (2000) suggests that, in her study, students with deeper understandings read more widely; they have a broader information universe. Lupton (2004) indicates that students with less sophisticated learning approaches constrain their information environment, whereas those with more complex experiences use a broader range of sources and enjoy resources that communicate well.

Investigations into how undergraduate and postgraduate students learn to program (Bruce, Buckingham, Hynd, McMahon, Roggenkamp, & Stoodley, 2006) provide another example suggesting that this may be the case. While this study did not specifically investigate information used, we may infer that the changing contexts within which the students see themselves as working have strong implications for the contents of their information worlds. For example, where the students see their work as contained within the learning institution, they rely heavily on information provided to them in the form of assigned tasks, lecture notes, and other study materials. Where students see the programming language they are learning as framing their experience, then information and resources pertaining to that language may be relevant; however, as the act of programming is experienced as coding, mostly they rely on software-generated messages to improve their code. Where students see themselves as participating in the programming community, then a wider range of resources comes into play. Where programming is experienced as satisfying clients, then their information horizons will extend further to incorporate those needs.

Encouraging students to widen their information horizons may be helped by emphasizing personal and professional relevance in course design (through the Personal Relevance frame), and by helping students to see that their use of information impacts on others (seventh face of informed learning).

Informed Learning Is Reflective and Critical

Becoming an informed learner involves becoming aware of the different ways of experiencing information use for learning through engaging in relevant research practices and reflection. The three critical elements in learning to be an informed learner (Bruce, 2002, p. 14) are:

- Coming to experience the different ways of using information to learn (learning)
- Reflecting on experience (being aware of learning)
- Applying the experience to novel contexts (transfer of learning)

The earlier chapters of this book focused on the different experiences and critical aspects of those experiences that are associated with informed learning. The next part of this chapter attends more closely to the second element of the learning process, reflecting on experience.

Reflection is integral to the experience of informed learning. The purpose of reflection is to focus learners' attention on important aspects of relevant information-use experiences. Reflective strategies may be designed based on models emerging from research. Students may be introduced to the models and asked to respond in their reflection to questions based on different parts of the models or simply to respond to the different parts of the models in their thinking and writing.

Merging Descriptions of Experience With Action Research Frameworks to Promote Reflection

Reflective models can be constructed from learning experiences through merging research outcomes with the action research—plan, act, record and reflect—framework. The action research framework is a well-accepted learning heuristic, which sits comfortably with our natural ways of working and also with many design and research processes. Integrating the action research framework with descriptions of the experience of information use produces models that assist the design of informed learning. Such models combine the principles of reflective practice, information literacy, and action research in frameworks that provide a theoretical basis for fostering critical approaches to information use and learning. They may be used with and by learners to scaffold learning and research progress. While students' reflective responses might be restricted by language limitations, cultural dissonance, and interpersonal uncertainty, simple frameworks can also help accommodate widespread diversity.

In these models, reflection is usually represented as one component of the action research cycle. The act of reflection is not, however, restricted to that part of the cycle. Because reflection is integral to the other components of the cycle, it forms a unifying thread throughout each model.

Similarly, while the models have a cyclic appearance, they are the essence of a network or web of interactions that support information.

The action research cycle has, for example, been brought together with ways of thinking and learning about the Internet (Edwards & Bruce, 2002, p. 183). Using this model (see Figure 4.4), students can be encouraged to think deeply about the processes of planning, acting, recording, and reflecting in light of our research insights into the experience of Internet searching.

Figure 4.4 Reflective model for learning to search the Internet (Edwards & Bruce, 2002, used with permission)

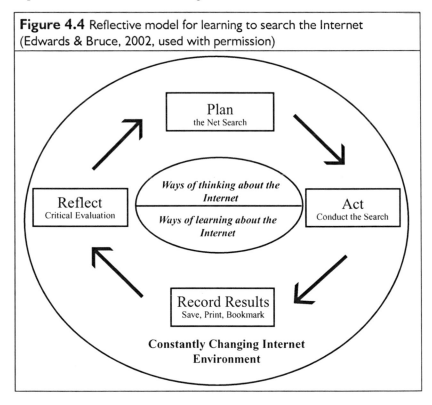

Suggestions for Learning Design

Based on the reflective model for learning to search the Internet, students could be asked questions such as the following:

As you complete learning task, describe

- how you planned your learning strategies, including your Internet searching;

- how you implemented your plans and any challenges you encountered;
- what you learned as you implemented the plans;
- how you kept records about your searching and your learning;
- what you learned through the act of record keeping.

Blending Models of Experience to Promote Informed Learning.

Different models can be brought together to form new models to promote the learning experience. For example, the reflective model for learning to search the Internet (see figure 4.4 above) has been integrated with the Seven Faces of Informed Learning to produce a model of reflective online information use (Hughes, Bruce, & Edwards, 2007; see figure 4.5 below). This model, in accordance with the action research cycle on which it is based, represents the dynamic and simultaneous nature of informed learning and proposes a holistic engagement with the ever-changing online information universe.

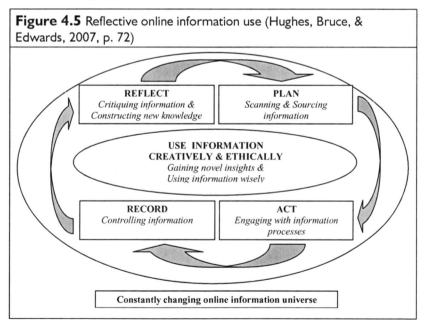

Figure 4.5 Reflective online information use (Hughes, Bruce, & Edwards, 2007, p. 72)

Hughes, Bruce, & Edwards (2007, p. 73) describe the alignment of the Seven Faces with the online information–use model as establishing recursive and nonlinear phases of information use so that "Learners are able to engage flexibly with information and they may pass through part or all of the meta-cycle once, several or many times depending on their information needs ... learners may jump phases, back track or exit midway." (p. 74). Similarly, the act of reflection is not confined to what may be described as the evaluative phase of the cycle "critiquing information and constructing new knowledge." For example, students may be encouraged to reflect on all other parts of the search process.

In this model, information use is central and is the focus as students go about planning, acting, recording, and reflecting. If students are oriented towards information use, then the model becomes a simultaneous learning model rather than a cyclic one (see discussion of Mandy Lupton's work earlier in this chapter).

Building Reflection into Assessment to Strengthen Informed Learning

Understanding students' experiences of engaging with the information environment can help us to develop assessment practices that encourage more complex approaches to informed learning. It is possible to move from an understanding of students' experience to assessment evaluation and redesign. The key is to focus students' attention appropriately and to help them see the different possible ways of focusing.

For example, Sylvia Edwards (2006, see details above) shows how learners using simpler approaches to Web searching are attending to fewer aspects of the search and learning process. They are focused on the topic, and yet are unaware of the structure of the Web environment and of the need to plan, reflect, and take into account the quality of resources. These students need to be encouraged to bring planning, reflection, and evaluation into focus. Similarly, students who do have a high level of awareness of more elements in the environment may be helped to consolidate their learning by bringing these to their attention through assessment.

The ways of seeing identified by Sylvia Edwards can be used to evaluate existing assessment instruments and strengthen them to improve students' searching experience (Edwards & Bruce, 2004). Assessment instruments fostering the search experience need to require engagement in the more complex approaches, for example asking students to discuss what features of a search engine they chose to use and why, or what databases they chose to search and why. They also need to ask students to focus on the important elements of the more complex categories, in this case the elements of reflecting, planning, and filtering their results.

Suggestions for Learning Design

Students could be asked to submit their five most important sources retrieved, together with an explanation of how these were selected, a discussion of what they learned from the resources, and a description of how they learned to filter their searches to retrieve a smaller number of higher quality results. The primary intention of assessment and feedback should be to move students towards the fourth experience.

Key Questions Arising From This Chapter—What Can We as Educators Do to Take This Agenda Further?

This chapter has delved more deeply into students' perspectives of informed learning. In order to help students learn, we need to establish deeper understandings of their experience and to encourage them towards desirable experiences.

Informed Learning and Your Philosophy of Teaching
- Why might it important to understand your students' experiences of informed learning?

Informed Learning and Your Students
- What are your students' experiences of the information practices you are bringing to their attention?
- How can you help your students discover these information practices for themselves?
- How can you design learning tasks to help students adopt the full range or the preferred ways of experiencing the practice?

Informed Learning and Your Curriculum Practice
- How do your students experience informed learning or information literacy in your course, program, or discipline?

- How do your students understand their experience of information practices, aspects of the information environment, or the relationship between information use and learning?
- How can our existing knowledge be used to aid learning in other disciplines?
- How can we use reflection to further aid learning in this domain? What other models are required to aid learners and curriculum designers?

References

Bruce, C. S. (2002). Information literacy as a catalyst for educational change: A background paper. White paper prepared for UNESCO, the U.S. National Commission on Libraries and Information Science, and the National Forum on Information Literacy, for use at the Information Literacy, Meetings of Experts, Prague, The Czech Republic, September 2003 (pp. 1–17). [Retrieved October 7, 2006 from http://www.nclis.gov/libinter/infolitconf&meet/papers/bruce-fullpaper.pdf]

Bruce, C. S., Buckingham, L., Hynd, J., McMahon, C., Roggenkamp, M., & Stoodley, I. (2006). Ways of experiencing the act of learning to program: A phenomenographic study of introductory programming students at university. In C. Bruce et al. (Eds.), Transforming IT education: Promoting a culture of excellence (pp. 301–326). Santa Rosa, CA: Informing Science Press. Also available online from http://ISPress.org in full text.

Bruce, C. S., & Middleton, M. (1999). Implementing assessment by portfolio in a professional practice unit. 1999 Herdsa Annual Conference, Melbourne, Australia. http://www.herdsa.org.au/branches/vic/Cornerstones/author-frameset.html

Edwards, S. L. (2006). *Panning for gold: Information literacy and the net lenses model.* Blackwood, South Australia: Auslib Press.

Edwards, S. L., & Bruce, C. S. (2002). Reflective Internet searching: An action research model. *The Learning Organization: An International Journal, 9*(3/4), 180–188.

Edwards, S. L., & Bruce, C. S. (2004). The assignment that triggered change: Assessment and the relational learning model for generic capabilities. *Assessment and Evaluation in Higher Education, 29*(2), 141–158.

Hughes, H., Bruce, C., & Edwards, S. (2007). Models for reflection and learning: A culturally inclusive response to the information literacy imbalance. In S. Andretta, (Ed.), *Change and challenge: Information literacy for the 21st century* (pp. 59–84). Blackwood, South Australia: Auslib Press.

Limberg, L. (2000). Is there a relationship between information seeking and learning outcomes? In C. Bruce & P. Candy (Eds.), *Information literacy around the world: Advances in programs and research* (pp. 193–208). Riverina, New South Wales, Australia: Centre for Information Studies, Charles Sturt University.

Locke, R. A. (2007). Learning information literacy: Qualitatively different ways education students learn to find and use information. Draft results chapter. December 2007. MPhil in progress, Griffith University, Brisbane, Australia.

Lupton, M. (2004). *The learning connection: Information literacy and the student experience.* Blackwood; South Australia: AusLib Press.

Lupton, M. (2008) *Information literacy and learning.* PhD thesis. Brisbane, Australia: Queensland University of Technology. (Available at http://adt. library.qut.edu.au)

Maybee, C. (2006). Undergraduate perceptions of information use: The basis for creating user-centred student information literacy instruction. *The Journal of Academic Librarianship, 32*(1), 79–85.

Maybee, C. (2007). Understanding our student learners: A phenomenographic study revealing the ways that undergraduate women at Mills College understand using information. *Reference Services Review 35,* 452–462.

Chapter 5

Informed Learning in the Disciplines and Professions

Opening Narrative

How will Jane's and Steve's students use information after they gradu-ate, as early career professionals? As Steve and Jane begin to think more about their students' early years after their university course, they begin to develop an interest in discipline-based and professional information practices. While cross-disciplinary insights have been useful, these need to be supplemented by deeper understandings of information practice in particular areas. Steve and Jane do not find a great deal in their own dis-ciplines, but they do find several examples from other creative, technical, and business domains. These examples reveal aspects of information that may be adaptable to their areas also.

To strengthen their understanding of their own disciplines, Steve and Jane decide to delve further into their own experience and talk with their colleagues, including their industry partners, about information prac-tices in their own fields. Once they have begun to explore the area and to apply it to their teaching, they find that they have material that may be of interest to others. It seems that there is a possibility of writing about their learning design and students' experiences of it for conferences and in journals focused on teaching and learning in their disciplines. These domain-specific examples may also help them to convince colleagues of the value of what they are doing.

Informed learning is grounded in disciplinary and professional information practices. In this chapter, I review research into informa-tion literacy in discipline-specific or professional contexts, providing a smorgasbord of ideas and insights from many fields. The chapter opens with academic perspectives of information literacy in selected disciplines. It then explores different experiences of information literacy and use in specific professions. Industry views of use of the Internet for information sharing, the information practices of auditors, senior managers' experiences of information literacy, and the experience of evidence-based practice all contribute to an emerging picture of the informed learning experience. The chapter goes on to explore the diverse experience of information in a range of disciplines and provides examples of curriculum design.

Informed Learning Is Grounded in Discipline and Professional Information Practices

Our disciplinary and professional informed learning experience lies at the heart of our activity as scholars, teachers, and researchers. And it is this experience that we should seek to bring to students, a prospect that requires us to think more about the information practices through which we learn. In some cases, we may be able to identify examples of the experience of such practices uncovered by researchers interested in information use and learning. Their findings may serve to direct and inspire those of us in the same discipline to look further at our own experience and to consider how we should form the learning and research experiences of our students.

For those of us from other disciplines, outcomes of these investigations serve as a guide and inspiration to examine and articulate our own experience in such a way that it may be shared with colleagues and with students. Perhaps in reading about the experiences of colleagues and reflecting on alternate approaches, our own experience may be enhanced, even cross-fertilized by strategies from other fields.

In the previous chapter, I expanded our understanding of informed learning by developing a picture of students' different ways of experiencing information literacy and their experience of certain academic information practices. In this chapter, I explore some examples available from research into the experience of information literacy in professional practice and in the context of specific disciplines. As in chapter 4, I am drawing together research focused on information literacy and information use under the banner of informed learning. Each research study is concerned with

Suggestions for Learning Design

Remember that in bringing the experiences described in this chapter to student learning, we may either be encouraging a subset of these experiences or be helping students grasp the full repertoire of the experiences. The various studies represented in this chapter may also provide inspiration for classroom-based research.

academics or professionals using information to learn. I also provide examples of how learning design might apply our growing understanding of information literacy in the disciplines and professions.

Informed Learning: The Experience of Discipline Experts

Why is it important to consider the experience of informed learning from the perspective of discipline experts, and how can the results be used? Delving deeply into the character of information use in our disciplines can provide significant inspiration for curriculum design. Susan Elrod and Mary Somerville, for example, inspired by the informed learning agenda, have developed a complete model for science curriculum to enculturate students into scientific information practices.

Learning Design: An Example of Informed Learning in Science

In the United States, Susan Elrod and Mary Somerville have designed Literature-Based Scientific Learning, which aims to advance discipline mastery and information literacy through giving students experience with the primary literature and engaging them in the scientific scholarly communication tradition. Their approach exemplifies informed learning as it facilitates discipline mastery through drawing scientific information processes into students' learning experiences.

The authors have taken up the challenge of bringing about learning through information use. Their intention is to "enculturate future scientists and engineers … into the cultural traditions of scientific enquiry. In furthering students' knowledge production capabilities, the aim was to advance both discipline mastery and information competence through employing a constructivist learning approach."

The strategy for implementing this approach was to develop literature-based case studies. From these case studies, students discussed researchers' contemporary scientific understanding, considered the data being worked with, and evolved questions that they then pursued though further engagement with the scientific literature. In this approach, students are encouraged to use at least the Information Sources and Knowledge Construction faces of informed learning. The teaching team could be said to be using the Learning to Learn and Relational frames for informed learning (Elrod & Somerville, 2007).

What does the experience of informed learning look like from the perspective of academics in particular disciplines? This is an important question because it is academics' own experiences that are often woven into the experiences they plan for their students. All of us, as teachers and researchers, have our own ways of interacting with information, which we potentially bring to learning design. Understanding our information interactions better will help us to articulate them to our students as we work towards enculturating them into our own community of practice.

A series of investigations have been conducted in the United Kingdom by Sheila Webber, Bill Johnston, and Stuart Boon, which have begun to provide insights into academics' perspectives in four different fields: English, marketing, chemistry and civil engineering. In these studies, the academics interviewed were asked to talk about their view of information literacy. The results available from the first three of these disciplines reveal idiosyncrasies between disciplines and also reveal similarities with and divergences from the Seven Faces of Informed Learning described in chapter 3. This compatibility suggests that the interdisciplinary and discipline-specific frameworks can work together in learning design.

English Academics' Experiences of Information Literacy
English academics' ways of experiencing information literacy (Boon, Johnston, & Webber, 2007) are summarized below. The first two ways of experiencing information literacy appear to bring together the Information Sources and Information Control faces of informed learning. The Information Control face has a strong element of establishing connections between a specific project or purpose and relevant resources, which is reflected by the research purpose aspects of the accessing and using ICT experiences. The third experience of English academics shares some similarities with the Information Process and Knowledge Construction faces of informed learning. Their fourth experience resembles the Wisdom face of informed learning, where the emphasis is on benefiting the wider community.

- *Accessing and Retrieving Textual Information*
In this experience, English academics focus on a specific research purpose, such as preparing a journal manuscript, and the resources involved

are conventionally static text or print, for example, books and journal or magazine articles.

- *Using ICT to Access and Retrieve Information*

In this experience, English academics focus on a specific research purpose; however, the required resources are not traditional, but are usually electronic or dynamic text, perhaps taking the form of online material, radio or television broadcasts, or other multimedia.

- *Possessing Basic Research Skills and Knowing When and How to Use Them*

In this experience, English academics focus on research capabilities and the ability to apply them in academic or professional contexts. Both traditional and nontraditional resources are important in this experience, particularly those made available through library infrastructure.

- *Becoming Confident Autonomous Learners and Thinkers*

In this experience, English academics focus on "personal growth and development and the acquisition of higher order information skills" (Boon, Johnston, & Webber, 2007, p. 218) to be able to contribute to or engage with the information society as members of an informed citizenry. Both traditional and nontraditional resources are important here.

Marketing Academics' Experiences of Information Literacy

Marketing academics' different ways of experiencing information literacy (Webber, Boon, & Johnston, 2005) are summarized below. The first two ways of experiencing information literacy appear to reflect the Information Awareness and Information Sources faces of informed learning. The third and fourth experiences of marketing academics tease apart elements of the Information Process face of informed learning. The Information Process face of informed learning fuses the use of information skills for problem solving or decision making. The fifth experience of marketing academics, focused on critical thinking, shares similarities with the Knowledge Construction face of informed learning.

The heavy reliance on information practices in marketing is highlighted by one of academics interviewed for the project: "Marketing is all about looking at information, from consumers and businesses, from governments and from consumer groups. It's all about making sense of data and information and then using that data to market a product, a company or an event" (Webber, Boon, & Johnston, 2005, p. 13). Being an effective, creative, and reflective information user is clearly an integral and essential part of being a professional marketer.

- *Accessing Information Quickly and Easily*

In this experience, marketing academics focus on awareness of, access to, and gathering of information. Marketing academics see the need to stay in touch with events and other relevant occurrences. Information sources are an important element of this experience.

- *Using IT to Work With Information*

In this experience, marketing academics focus on using information technology efficiently and effectively to work with information. Relevant application software that enables communication, manipulation, and analysis are important elements of this experience.

- *Possessing a Set of Information Skills and Applying Them to the Task in Hand*

In this experience, marketing academics focus on developing a suite of individual skills and being able to apply them to an information task or practice. Skills such as accessing, sorting, analyzing, and disseminating information are highlighted as important elements of this experience.

- *Using Information to Solve Real-World Problems*

In this experience, marketing academics focus on understanding problems and how information can be used to solve problems.

- *Becoming a Critical Thinker*

In this experience, marketing academics focus on applying critical thinking to information processes. Higher-order skills, such as understanding and interpreting information, and adopting a questioning approach are emphasized as important elements of this experience.

- *Becoming a Confident Independent Practitioner*

In this experience, marketing academics focus on using information effectively in order to develop personal professional confidence. Marketers using information this way are able to make sense of and work with information in professional practice.

Learning Design: An Example of Marketing Students Using Professional Information Practices

An early experiment in bringing workplace information practices into the curriculum was undertaken by Morrison and Stein (1999) at the University of Delaware. Morrison, a professor of consumer studies, and Stein, a librarian at the university, worked together to require students to use information available via the World Wide Web in making business decisions. Senior students from different courses in global telecommunications and marketing in the global economy worked in groups, forming "marketing research teams." They were asked to synthesize information in order to determine "whether a small-town sports minded business ... should adopt a posture of marketing by means of the WWW" (p. 319). As part of the learning process, students were asked to evaluate four different strategies for contemporary information gathering and problem solving (p. 321). Despite the student-centered, information-rich learning environment provided, Morrison and Stein found that the students were not effective in sourcing high-quality, credible information.

What insights could be applied from the Six Frames and Seven Faces to this case reported in the literature?
It seems that, in this example, Morrison and Stein were providing a learning experience that encouraged self-direction and was of high relevance to the students. (We could say they were adopting the Learning to Learn and Personal Relevance frames.) In terms of facilitating informed learning, they appear to have been primarily adopting the Information Sources face, allowing students freedom in their choice of approach to searching and providing the guidance of an information professional, especially a librarian. The overall result may have been strengthened if students had been required to *compare the results of their own choices with the results of professionally guided searching;* or if the fifth face of informed learning, *emphasizing critical thinking and evaluation strategies* in the knowledge-construction process, had received more explicit attention.

Chemistry Academics' Experiences of Information Literacy
Chemistry academics' ways of experiencing information literacy (Webber & Johnston, 2007) are summarized below. The first of chemistry academics' ways of experiencing information literacy reflects the Information Awareness aspect of the first face of informed learning. The second of their experiences reflects the Information Process face of informed learning. The third experience of chemistry academics appears

to fuse aspects of the Information Awareness and Knowledge Extension faces of informed learning. Their fourth experience resembles the Wisdom face of informed learning, where the emphasis is on benefiting the wider community.

- *Searching Chemical Information*

In this experience, chemists see themselves as information consumers: They are primarily concerned with published chemical information or data. Their information literacy expertise is applied in specific courses or projects.

- *Mastering Chemists' Information Skill Set*

In this experience, chemists see themselves as information consumers and engage in practical application of that information. Their information world consists of published chemical information and the data that they create or work with. Their information literacy expertise is applied in the broader world of chemistry.

- *Communicating Scientific Information*

In this experience, chemists see themselves as consumers and creators of information. Their expertise in applied in the workplace, including the chemistry domain.

- *An Essential Part of the Constitution of Knowledge*

In this experience, chemists see themselves as information consumers, creators, and advocates. Their expertise is additionally applied in the broader social context.

Professional Experiences of Informed Learning

The following three examples, rather than being discipline-specific, reveal aspects of how information is used as groups or individuals learn in professional life. Each example reflects the everyday experiences of the participants' working lives. The first looks at information literacy as experienced by senior managers. The second looks at experience of an information practice, construction industry workers' use of the Internet for sharing information. The third investigates information professionals' views of evidenced-based practice. Examples such as these can provide research-based professional examples of informed learning that could influence learning design. All three examples reveal the different foci associated with each experience, making it possible for teachers to encourage students to use the relevant lenses.

Senior Managers' Experiences of Information Literacy
Joyce Kirk (2004) interviewed senior managers in public sector organizations in order to understand variation in their experience of information.
These managers were responsible for organizational strategy and performance. Their experience of information use, which shows similarities
with the more generalized picture we have of information use in the
Seven Faces of Informed Learning, may be summarized as follows.

- *Information Use Seen as Packaging Information*

When experiencing information use this way, managers focus on their
active, physical manipulation of information "getting information in,
manipulating it, getting it out." An example might be securing and
then arranging information under relevant headings required for a
report. In this experience, the quality of information and the audience
for whom it is designed take high priority. While the presentation of
the final package is often seen as formulaic, this is not always the case.
This experience shares similarities with the Information Sources and
Information Control faces of informed learning.

- *Information Use Seen as Enabling the Flow of Information*

When information use is seen this way, information is shared or com-
municated among a group in the context of an observable activity, such
as a workshop or information-sharing discussion. Managers experiencing information use this way focus on those channels that encourage
information flow and possible impediments. They are keenly interested
in ensuring information exchange. This experience shares similarities
with the Information Process face of informed learning.

- *Information Use Seen as Developing New Knowledge and Insights*

In contrast with the "packaging" experience, managers seeing this way
focus on the "conceptual and cerebral." "Analysis and reflection, thinking and learning dominate the process" (p. 195). Physical separation
from the organization was sometimes preferred to reflect on unique or
innovative approaches. Relevant information sources in this experience
varied from people to Internet discussions, documents, and archives.
This experience involves recognizing changing thinking as bringing
about risks and unknown territory, as well as challenging traditional
workplace and professional practices. This experience shares similarities with the Knowledge Construction and Knowledge Extension faces
of informed learning.

- *Information Use Seen as Shaping Judgments and Decisions*

When seeing this way, managers rely on intuition and see themselves as being on a journey involving two interdependent processes: "verification of the information on which judgments and decisions were based through desk research and conversations with trusted colleagues, and confirmation of the appropriateness of the judgments and decisions as they were emerging, again through conversations with trusted colleagues and others …" (p. 195). This experience shares similarities with the Information Process face of informed learning.

- *Information Use Seen as Influencing Others*

When seeing this way, managers are engaged in a major change process, using information to precipitate and bring about that change. The information-use process commences with the recognition of the need for change and is seen as concluding when evidence of change is visible. Internal and external information, as well as observations of peoples' behavior, are important to them. This experience shares similarities with the Wisdom face of informed learning.

- *Experiences of Using the Internet for Information Sharing in the Construction Industry*

In recent years, the Internet has become a site of information practice in many industries. An in-depth exploration of the use of the Internet for sharing information on major construction projects (Magub, 2006) shows that such use of the Internet may be experienced in different ways, each associated with its own distinctive focus. The people interviewed for this research worked in different parts of the world, mostly using the Internet as a primary vehicle for communicating with each other. The outcomes show that informed learning in professional settings is bound up with the workplace and industry culture. The experiences described here appear to amplify the Information Awareness and Communication and the Information Control faces of informed learning.

- *Using the Internet for Information Sharing Experienced as Using an Efficient, Easy-to-Use Communications Tool*

When experiencing using the Internet for sharing information this way, staff focus on perceived advantages, such as the currency of information, accessibility of data, efficiency of communication, and minimal need for training, as well as the need for openness and accountability. The Internet itself is not of primary concern. Staff using this lens are positive about their experience of project communication and participation.

- *Using the Internet for Information Sharing Experienced as Using a Flexible Tool to Help Save Resources*

When experiencing using the Internet for sharing information this way, staff focus on the ability to monitor the performance of project participants and the reduction of certain project costs associated with Internet use, for example, the reduced cost of production of paper copies. The ability of project staff to work remotely and transfer project data is also important. Use of the Internet for communication is somewhat in the background. Staff using this lens are positive about their experience of project communication and participation.

- *Using the Internet for Information Sharing Experienced as Having a Competitive Advantage in an Industrywide Trend*

When experiencing using the Internet for sharing information this way, staff focus on the "competitive advantage" gained by their activity, as well as on trends in this direction across the industry. Sharing information through the Internet places the organization in a privileged position, working and communicating across geographical boundaries. Staff using this lens are positive about their experience of project communication and participation.

- *Using the Internet for Information Sharing Experienced as Using a Reliable Centralized Data Archive*

When experiencing using the Internet for sharing information this way, staff focus on archival elements, with the Internet itself being somewhat in the background of awareness. The primary advantage experienced here is the availability of a single place for depositing project information that has powerful archival and search-and-retrieval features. The use of a single system allows geographically dispersed project teams to be efficient and to maintain a high level of organization despite the growing volume of project information. Staff using this lens are neutral about their experience of project communication and participation.

- *Using the Internet for Information Sharing Experienced as Using Another Communications Tool*

When experiencing sharing information via the Internet this way, staff focus on all forms of communication. In this experience, information sharing via the Internet is simply one of a range of project communications options and is less important than people and processes to the success of projects. Face-to-face communications have a high value when Internet use is experienced this way, and other forms of communication are necessary because of the limitations of IT. Staff using this lens are neutral about their experience of project communication and participation.

• *Using the Internet for Information Sharing Experienced as a Multiplier of Communication and Documentation*

When experiencing sharing information via the internet this way, staff focus on the potential multiplier effect of Internet communication, with considerably more copies being generated as part of the communication process than would otherwise be the case. Often these communications are seen as unnecessary. The information system is also regarded as operating alongside other, paper-based systems, again bringing about duplication of materials and systems. Staff using this lens are negative about their experience of project communication and participation.

• *Using the Internet for Information Sharing Experienced as a Barrier to Effective Project Participation*

Here, project staff see use of the Internet for information sharing as a barrier to working on the project team. When experiencing sharing information via the Internet this way, staff focus on technology that is perceived as interfering with the process, and the strength of the barrier is increased. For example, the speed and quality of the Internet connection may be an issue, as may be team members' difficulties in learning how to use the system. Physical barriers, such as scanning capability, may also be an issue preventing certain project data from being incorporated in the system. Costs of these issues to the project then become notable. Staff using this lens are negative about their experience of project communication and participation.

Information Professionals Engaged in Informed Learning: Their Experience of Evidence-Based Practice

Evidence-based practice is an example of a professional information practice that may already be a part of curriculum. Insights into the different lenses brought to evidence-based practice could be used to encourage learners to adopt those experiences suited to their contexts. We should remember that, as teachers, we need to make a professional

Learning Design: An Example of Engineering Students Forming Virtual Work Teams

An engineering course using problem-based learning approaches in Australia (Gibbings & Brodie, 2008, in press) adopts a practice closely related to the idea of using the Internet for information sharing. The course creates an environment where e-mail, discussion boards, synchronous chat sessions, and other methods of communication typically used in professional contexts are an integral part of students' learning experiences. The students, most of whom are studying in distance mode, are asked to form virtual teams for the purposes of completing projects; they are also asked to use allocated discussion boards to facilitate communication within each group. Additionally, after having worked together for a short while, groups are allowed to choose for themselves their preferred strategies for communication.

This aspect of students' processes reflects the first of the Seven Faces of Informed Learning and is being implemented in accordance with the principles derived from Seven Faces that user preferences should be respected and that information use is a social, rather than an individual, experience. The teaching team could be said to be using a combination of Learning to Learn and Personal Relevance as their primary frames.

judgment about which forms of experience to encourage so that students can, in future, choose to adopt the categories most appropriate to their context.

Evidence-based practice is a vehicle for informed learning used widely across the health, education, information, and other professions. Partridge, Thorpe, and Edwards (2007) reveal that information professionals have four different ways of experiencing evidence-based practice. Each of these is very much about the kinds of information that are admitted as "evidence" and also establish the focal concerns in each experience.

Evidence-Based Practice Experienced as a Professional Accident
Here professionals focus on "doing my job" and on their self-reliance within the work context. They see themselves as engaging in evidence-

based practice without knowing anything about what it is. The expertise of others is used or drawn upon only when required; change is reactive and driven by the larger corporate context. Evidence is gathered only to support decision making; evidence is considered to be data obtained through surveys or experiments, which are conducted when decisions are required.

Evidence-Based Practice Experienced as Learning From and Using Research
Here professionals focus on demonstrating their value to the organization. They see themselves as needing to justify their professional approaches or activities by referring to accepted research outcomes. When experiencing evidence-based practice this way, reviewing the literature and using the published outputs of others are preferred to conducting original or context-specific empirical research.

Evidence-Based Practice Experienced as an Activity Undertaken to Improve Professional Service
Here professionals focus on identifying, achieving, and implementing best practice. Evidence-based practice is applied on a "project" basis; however, practitioners rely on themselves in non-project tasks. Implementation of projects is highly structured, with goals and milestones to monitor achievements, and research is conducted within this framework.

Evidence-Based Practice Experienced as All-Consuming, Seamlessly Permeating All Professional Practice
Here professionals focus on being a receiver and manager of evidence. An evidence-based approach is seen as the essence of professional existence. The professional constantly receives feedback or information from clients and colleagues and is responsible for processing and acting upon that evidence in a proactive way. The implementation of new strategies may be unstructured or haphazard, with strategies often evolving organically.

More on Information Literacy in the Professions and Disciplines
There are many examples of investigations into the ways in which different disciplines and professions interact with information, including a

range of emerging studies into professional and workplace experiences of information literacy. The examples I have highlighted in this chapter so far target significant differences in experience and are therefore ideally suited to learning design based on a relational approach.

Other studies, while not targeting significant differences in experience, do provide rich pictures of information literacy in different professional or discipline contexts. Annemaree Lloyd (2007), for example, has investigated information literacy among firefighters, Christine Brown (2002) reports on music scholars engaged in the research process, and Kautto and Talja (2007) have investigated how evaluating the scholarly literature is learned in specific disciplines. Some journals that report such investigations include *The New Review of Information Behaviour Research, Studies of Information Seeking in Context,* and *Library and Information Science Research.*

Auditors Engaged in Informed Learning

Bonnie Cheuk (2000), for example, explores the information practices of auditors. She finds that the broad information process usually involves

- planning how information will be sought and used, as well as presenting those plans via a memorandum;
- gathering background information about the company being audited;
- consulting information sources such as annual reports and previous audit reports;
- undertaking the audit in the field and working with relevant on-site information such as company files, minutes, and financial statements;
- conducting an exit meeting;
- reporting (adapted from p. 182).

One of Cheuk's primary findings is that professional information practices are not solely the domain of the individual. She points out that individuals' information processes are part of a chain where the information produced or managed by one person may be used by a different person at another time. She also highlights that, for auditors, required information is often provided, rather than sought; information seeking is not a systematic process, often happening by trial and error; and obtaining necessary information does not always mean the successful completion of a task.

Cheuk concludes that, for auditors, information use is not an orderly or systematic process, but rather a creative, diverse, and personal process. It is also not a rigid process with guidelines and steps to be followed, but rather is seen as a flexible, creative, and reflective thinking process used to decide what steps to take. Her findings reflect closely those of the Seven Faces of Informed Learning (chapter 3), where experience from a range of different professions and disciplines emphasizes the importance of *personal heuristics and personal creativity* in information use.

Informed Learning Accepts the Diverse Forms That Information Might Take

Information is not only that which is accessible from formal or informal sources such as databases or discussion forums. Information can be anywhere, anytime—it needs to be identified as *informing*, as something that contributes to our increasing awareness of the world. We need to learn to recognize information that is relevant to our practice. Textual information is becoming less stable, more fluid, as the information environment is increasingly digitized and is made available via a World Wide Web that has the capacity to deal with sound, graphics, video, and a wide range of interactive experiences. How do people experience information? Information is experienced as that which informs. It can be experienced as objective, subjective, or transformational (Bruce, 1997). Such an approach fuses traditional separations between data, information, and knowledge; recorded and unrecorded knowledge or information. In such an approach, there is no need to conceptually separate information and knowledge; there is no need to represent them as part of a hierarchy.

In informing, information makes a contribution to something larger—it becomes part of a process that determines action, enables insights, creates a work of art. The sound of rain informs a musician in one way, has a different meaning for a choreographer, a dancer, or a child at play. That which informs may take the form of any medium—it may be a physical artifact or sound; textual, visual, or embodied. Musicians, for example, may be informed by images, sounds, or feelings (Lupton, 2008), firefighters may be informed by their own bodily responses and reactions, as well as those of their colleagues (Lloyd & Somerville, 2006).

Exploring the experience of information use provides some insight into the many forms that information might take in different disciplines and professional contexts. Table 5.1 summarizes a few of these that have been documented through a range of research projects. While most of this chapter has focused on information use in different professions and disciplines, the diverse forms of information highlight for us the need to continually review what constitutes information in our field.

Table 5.1 The character of information for different communities of practice.

Community of Practice	Forms of Information
Generic	Overall we note that information may take many forms: textual, visual, aural, affective, kinesthetic or embodied; and varies with the discipline or community of practice involved (Lupton and Bruce, manuscript). "Information is all around us. Our senses collect and our brains filter and organize information every minute of the day. At a very fundamental level information colors our perceptions of the world around us, and thereby influences attitudes, emotions and actions." (Rowley, 1998).
Firefighters	Information for firefighters includes embodied information, their bodies and those of their colleagues convey information. For this group, the fire itself is information (Lloyd & Somerville, 2006).
Auditors	Information for auditors is not...homogenous for auditors as a group, but can be different for each individual...(Cheuk, 2000).
Music composition students	Information for music composition students includes sound samples, the acoustic qualities of sound, feeling sound, creating the sound, music theory, composers' techniques and characteristics, the students' and the composers' thoughts, experiences, attitudes, and beliefs (Lupton, 2008).
Tax law students	Information for tax law students includes techniques, such as mind mapping and legal research; a cyclic process of finding and using information, texts such as legislation, case law, articles, bills; viewpoints of others or the students' own viewpoints; clients' situation and needs; the students' personal situation or needs (Lupton, 2008).

School principals	Information for school principals reviewing the performance of new teachers includes: interviews, body language, student behavior in the classroom, feedback from parents and department heads, dress, extra-curricular and community involvement (Ballantyne, Thompson, & Taylor, 1994).
Construction staff	Information for construction projects includes drawings, e-mail correspondence, minutes of meetings, workflow, requests for information, submissions, contracts (Magub, 2006).
Bakers	Information for bakers includes bread making knowledge and recipes, food safety, equipment upgrades, workplace health and safety legislation, payroll and tax considerations, council and government regulations and laws, and industry innovations. This may be obtained from a franchisee, councils, industry representatives or the Internet (Smith & Matina, 2004).
Marketing academics	Information for marketing academics includes textual and numeric information, business information, newspapers, contacts feature in their description (Webber, Boon, & Johnston, 2005).
English academics	Information for English academics—texts/primary sources, books, journals, magazines, archives, broadcasts, web resources (Webber, Boon, & Johnston, 2005).

Key Questions Arising From This Chapter—What Can We as Educators Do to Take This Agenda Further?

Informed Learning and Your Philosophy of Teaching

- What aspects of informed learning are important to you as a discipline specialist or professional practitioner?
- What information practices are important to you as a discipline specialist or professional practitioner?
- What forms of information are important to you as a discipline specialist or professional practitioner?
- Which of the above would be important to build into your students' learning experiences?

Informed Learning and Your Students
- How do your students experience relevant discipline or professional information practices?
- How do your students experience relevant forms of information?

Informed Learning and Your Curriculum Practice
- What information experiences or practices do you believe should be incorporated into your curriculum?
- What do you already do to engage your students with relevant forms of information or information practices?
- How could you further build relevant experiences of information or information practices into students' learning experiences?

Informed Learning in Your Field
- How do members of your discipline experience information use or specific practices?
- What ways of experiencing information or information literacy are vital to your profession or discipline?
- What information practices capture these experiences?
- What forms does information take in your field?

References

Ballantyne, R, Thompson, R., & Taylor, P. (1994). Principals' conceptions of competent beginning teachers. In R. Ballantyne & C. Bruce (Eds.), *Phenomenography: Philosophy and practice. Proceedings, Brisbane, Australia: Queensland University of Technology, 7–9 Nov,* 23–45.

Boon, S., Johnston, B., & Webber, S. (2007). A phenomenographic study of English faculty's conceptions of information literacy. *Journal of Documentation, 63*(2), 204–228.

Brown, C. D. (2002). Straddling the humanities and social sciences: The research process of music scholars. *Library and Information Science Research, 24*(1), 73–94.

Bruce, C. S. (1997). *The seven faces of information literacy.* Blackwood, South Australia: AusLib Press.

Cheuk, B. (2000). Exploring information literacy in the workplace: A process approach. In C. Bruce & P. Candy (Eds.), *Information literacy around the world: Advances in programs and research* (pp. 177–192). Riverina, Australia: Centre for Information Studies, Charles Sturt University.

Elrod, S., & Somerville, M. (2007). Literature Based Scientific Learning: A collaboration model. *Journal of Academic Librarianship, 33*, 684–691.

Gibbings, P., & Brodie, L. (in press, 2008). Learning communities in virtual space. *International Journal of Engineering Education.*

Kautto, V., & Talja, S. (2007). Disciplinary socialization: Learning to evaluate the quality of scholarly literature. *Advances in Library Administration and Organization 25*, 33–59.

Kirk, J. (2004). Tumble dryers and juggernauts: Information-use processes in organisations. In *Lifelong learning: Whose responsibility and what is your contribution? Refereed papers from the 3rd Lifelong Learning Conference, Yeppoon, Australia, 13–16 June 2004*, pp. 192–197. http://lifelonglearning.cqu.edu.au/2004/papers

Lloyd, A. (2007). Learning to put out the red stuff: Becoming information literate through discursive practice. *Library Quarterly, 77*(2), 181–198.

Lloyd, A., & Somerville, M. (2006). Working information. *Journal of Workplace Learning,, 18*(3), 186–198.

Lupton, M. (2008) *Information literacy and learning.* PhD thesis. Brisbane, Australia: Queensland University of Technology. (Available at http://adt.library.qut.edu.au)

Lupton, M. and Bruce, C.S. (manuscript) Windows on information literacy worlds: The GeST model.

Magub, A. (2006). Experiences of the phenomenon of Internet use for information sharing on construction projects and skills set identification for effective project participation. PhD thesis. Brisbane, Australia: Queensland University of Technology. Available at http://adt.library.qut.edu.au/

Morrison, J. L., & Stein, L. L. (1999). Assuring integrity of information utility in cyber-learning formats. *Reference Services Review, 27*, 317–326.

Partridge, H., Thorpe, C., & Edwards, S. L. (2007). The practitioner's experience and conception of evidence based library and information practice: An exploratory analysis. Paper presented at the 4th International Evidence Based Library and Information Practice Conference, Chapel Hill–Durham, NC, USA. 6–11 May 2007. http://www.eblip4.unc.edu/papers/Partridge.pdf

Rowley, J. (1998). What is information? *Information Services and Use, 18*(4), 243–254.

Smith, E., & Matina, C. (2004). Keeping the dough rising: Information in the workplace with reference to the bakery trade, In *Lifelong learning: Whose responsibility and what is your contribution? Refereed papers from the 3rd Lifelong Learning Conference, Yeppoon, Australia, 13–16 June 2004*, pp. 325–329. http://lifelonglearning.cqu.edu.au/2004/papers

Webber, S., Boon, S., & Johnston, B. (2005). A comparison of UK academics' conceptions of information literacy in two disciplines: English and marketing. *Library and Information Research, 29*(93), 4–15.

Webber, S., & Johnston, B. (2007). Conceptions of information literacy of UK chemistry and English academics. Seminar presented at the Department of Information Studies, University of Sheffield, March 2007.

Chapter 6

Informed Learning in the Community and Workplace

Opening Narrative

Steve and Jane decide that they are going to try something new. Jane decides that a class will prepare a client briefing on the topic of water efficiency. The briefing will be written (a) for the management team of a child-care center wishing to enhance their efficiency in water use and (b) for the parents of children attending the child-care center. The briefing will include a synopsis of students' sources of information and why those sources were used. Steve decides that one of his classes will research the impact of the drought on suburbia and create a suite of artworks to display in local community centers.

Both Steve's and Jane's students' work will be going to a group of professionals for perusal, and their work will also inform the community. Jane's students will develop resources to inform parents and caregivers; Steve's students' art will inform the wider local community. As part of the learning experience, the students will work with members of both groups. What do the students need to know about the experience of informed learning in the workplace and in the community? What could the students learn about being informed learners in the community or workplace from this experience? Steve and Jane are now working with the Personal Relevance and Social Impact frames for informed learning. How could they use the Seven Faces of Informed Learning to help their students think through these issues as well?

In thinking about these issues, Steve and Jane take an interest in creative and reflective information use from a broader perspective and discover the GeST, windows, through which the information-use experience may theoretically be viewed. The situated and transformative windows are particularly interesting to them as their students' learning begins to cross community and workplace boundaries.

How can Steve's and Jane's students develop their work in recognition of what and how information is used in community and workplace settings?

Using information to learn is central not only in the disciplines and professions, but also in the wider context of workplace and community. As we extend students' learning experiences into workplace and community contexts, they have the opportunity to experience and reflect on informed learning in those settings. In this chapter, I introduce the GeST windows for considering informed learning in the workplace and the community. I explore the character of informed learning in the workplace and the community, adapting the Seven Faces model to suggest what the experience of informed learning might look like in those settings. This chapter invites exploration of what it may mean to prepare students to be informed learners in the community or workplace and to respond to workplace and community issues in their professional practice.

Informed Learning Supports Social Learning and Educational Partnerships in the Community and Workplace

Informed learning, particularly through the Personal Relevance and Social Impact frames, encourages us to design learning experiences that are situated in community and workplace contexts.

Engaging in informed learning in the workplace and community brings with it the opportunity to explore creative and reflective information use in real-world contexts, which tend to be less structured and subject to change. Learners engaged in community and workplace activity are likely to need to learn to recognize new forms of information and new ways of communicating that information. They will learn to take their formal experiences of learning into informal learning environments and begin to develop some appreciation of what it might take to be informed learners in those contexts. In working in community and workplace settings, students are likely to find that using their reflective capabilities will be crucial to influencing change. They will also find many similarities and synergies across the academic, workplace, and community contexts, particularly in relation to continuous change on social, cultural, and technological fronts.

As with specific professions and disciplines, the nature of information changes in workplace and community contexts. We must engage with an enormous, diverse, and fluid information environment, including people and their behavior, art, text, sound, and language, which today must be supplemented further with the proliferation of electronic communities and contexts. Perhaps the only constant among all these varied and changing environments is the human need for informed learning to flourish.

What might informed learning look like in the workplace and in the community? This chapter introduces the GeST windows as frames for thinking about informed learning across these sectors and explores the applicability of the Seven Faces of Informed Learning to both these settings. Exploring the character of informed learning in these settings suggests directions for learning experiences we might devise.

The GeST Windows

The GeST windows construct our possible consideration of information literacy as either generic, situated, or transformative (Lupton & Bruce, manuscript). They draw together the generic, situated, and transformative orientations to information literacy, hence their name.

Where the Six Frames for Informed Learning are designed specifically for formal educational purposes, the GeST windows have a broader applicability across sectors and are of special interest to those of us with a range of community and workplace concerns. The Six Frames are aligned with different curriculum orientations. The GeST windows orient us to information literacy as reflected by alternative world views: critical (the Transformative window), sociocultural (the Situated window), and behavioral (the Generic window). The GeST windows were derived from drawing on perspectives on literacy that also reflect these different world views, as well as from drawing on some elements of the Six Frames. Each of the three windows will be suited to different learning needs or workplace and community contexts in which students find themselves.

The Seven Faces of Informed Learning continue to serve as a working picture of the different ways in which informed learning is experienced. Their applicability to the community and workplace contexts is discussed in later parts of this chapter.

The Generic Window

Through the Generic window, information literacy is considered from a behavioral perspective. It is usually seen as being about competencies and skills. Information is external and objective. This view has sympathy with the Content and Competency frames of informed learning. The Generic window is displayed in Table 6.1.

Suggestion for Learning Design

Students will locate a set of Internet resources by following recommended processes and will evaluate those Internet resources according to a set of predetermined criteria.

Table 6.1 The Generic window (adapted from Lupton and Bruce, manuscript)

Information literacy is…	the cognitive skills and processes that individuals use for finding and managing information.
Information literacy is important because…	we need a flexible workforce to be competitive in a globalized, technologized world.
We find information by…	using search strategies.
We use information to…	evaluate, manage, and organize information.
Information consists of…	text and images that are accessed and managed via tools.
Information is regarded as…	external and objective.
Information is evaluated by…	examining currency, bias, authority, and provenance.
Information literacy is taught by…	practicing with search strategies, Internet evaluation checklists, and ICT skills; and citing and referencing in generic workshops and lectures.
Information literacy is learned by…	practicing search skills and following a series of stages.
Information literacy is assessed by…	standardized tests, including online tutorials.

The Situated Window

Through the Situated window, information literacy is considered from a sociocultural perspective. It is usually seen as being about contextualized information practices, socially constructed in the experience of the people engaged in those practices. Information is social and has different forms and different meanings for the people using it. The Situated window suggests learning about information use in context, in formal or informal learning environments. This view is sympathetic with the Learning to Learn frame for informed learning. The Situated window is displayed in Table 6.2.

Table 6.2 The Situated window (adapted from Lupton and Bruce, manuscript)

Information literacy is…	a range of contextualized information practices (discipline, work, family, or community).
Information literacy is important because…	we need to find and use information for personal, work, and community purposes.
We find information by…	asking people, observing people and phenomena, and using tools.
We use information to…	create new knowledge and solve problems.
Information consists of…	opinions, ideas, text, images, and aural, visual, affective, kinesthetic, and embodied stimuli
Information is regarded as…	internal and subjective.
Information is evaluated by…	examining multiple sources of information and how information is produced and communicated; and the social, historical, cultural, political, and economic context of information.
Information literacy is taught by…	providing authentic information practices in contextualized settings.
Information literacy is learned by…	engaging in authentic information practices.
Information literacy is assessed by…	the process and outcome of engaging in authentic information practices.

Suggestion for Learning Design

Students will review client cases and locate a set of Internet resources to meet clients' needs. They will evaluate those Internet resources according to how the resources fit with client requirements and will propose possible directions appropriate to the client's context.

The Transformative Window

Through the Transformative window, information literacy is considered from a critical perspective. It is usually seen as being about transforming oneself and society. Through this window, information literacy is both a catalyst for learning (Bruce, 2002) and a catalyst for social change. Information is seen as ideological, and information use may take on a political character. The Transformative window suggests learning that encourages social critique. Such critique should be tempered by recognition of the need for ethical and "other"-oriented approaches to information use, as described in the seventh (Wisdom) face of informed learning. This view is

Table 6.3 The Transformative window (adapted from Lupton and Bruce, manuscript)

Information literacy is…	adopting a range of ways of using information to transform oneself and society.
Information literacy is important because…	we need to be empowered to learn and bring about new ways of doing things in the world.
We find information by…	using a variety of lenses with which to view information and knowledge production.
We use information to…	question the status quo, challenge existing practice, and empower oneself and the community.
Information consists of…	anything that informs, especially the implicit and explicit meanings and assumptions inherent in textual and social practices.
Information is regarded as…	transformative.
Information is evaluated by…	examining whose interests are served, who is silent, inherent assumptions, how knowledge and information are produced, and what counts as knowledge.
Information literacy is taught by…	empowering learners to engage in information practices for the transformation of society.
Information literacy is learned by …	engaging in collaborative and participatory information practices that critique society and lead to social action.
Information literacy is assessed by …	the process and outcome of social critique and action.

sympathetic with the Social Impact and Personal Relevance frames for informed learning. The Transformative window is displayed in Table 6.3.

Suggestion for Learning Design

Students will collaborate with a social or work-based community to research and critique the status quo and to construct recommendations for future directions.

Informed learning in the community and workplace requires us to be familiar with all the windows. It is the Situated and Transformative windows, however, that are going to help learners find meaning and relevance and to go on to experience or be responsible for personal, professional, and social change as a result of their learning activities.

The following research example demonstrates how all three GeST windows can work together when the transformative aspects of information use are of primary importance. The example fuses workplace and community issues and shows how becoming advocates for change in the community can benefit from the combined adoption of all three orientations: generic, situated, and transformative.

Information Literacy Needs of Local Staff in Cross-Cultural Development Projects
Camille McMahon interviewed community development workers about what was required to help local workers with information literacy in cross-cultural contexts (McMahon & Bruce, 2002).

The investigation aimed to identify significant differences in development workers' ways of seeing information-related learning needs among local staff participating in community development projects in cross-cultural contexts. In this situation, learning involved gaining a voice and influencing developments for change, and the perceptions of information literacy–related learning needs identified are seen to be related to the Seven Faces of Informed Learning.

Key outcomes from the investigation were:

- A model of the IL needs of local workers in community development projects.
- Insights into the impact of introducing ICT in an environment where intended users are unfamiliar with the technology.

Some of these impacts stem from needs as basic as reading and writing skills.

- Identification of the need for a multilayered approach to meeting IL needs in cross-cultural contexts.
- Identification of the need for enhanced communication between western project managers and local workers about a wider range of issues around the project implementation experience

The model (see figure 6.1) identifies five different ways of experiencing information literacy related learning needs, with each experience including important elements of the preceding categories. Local workers, in order to use information to learn in their own cultural contexts, are seen as needing

- *Basic literacy skills.* Reading, writing, arithmetic, and speaking the language of the project provider are seen as important keys to being able to contribute within the mainstream culture or the dominant system brought by the development project. These basic literacy skills are regarded as a prerequisite to being able to use information to learn.

- *Understanding of workplace systems.* This includes (a) use of communications technologies, computers, phones, and e-mail, and (b) office systems and structures, such as forms, messaging, and record-keeping systems. All of these may be foreign concepts that need to be mastered, along with sensitivity to different cultural values and assumptions, in order to use information and participate in the new systems being developed. This need reflects the Information Awareness and Communication and Information Control faces of informed learning.

- *Communication skills.* Being able to use information requires the ability to communicate with colleagues in the project team and to communicate about the project to fellow members of the community affected. Critical to good communication is the ability to act as a cross-cultural translator, mediating between the local culture and the new approaches brought in by the development project. This need also reflects elements of the first face, Information Awareness and Communication, of informed learning.

- *Access to information sources.* This includes being able to source relevant information to meet project and community needs. This need reflects the Information Sources face of information learning.

- *Understanding of the dominant society.* In this experience, the primary need for using information to learn is the ability to understand the dominant culture, its values, and its assumptions. The dominant culture here is usually the culture of the funding provider and includes the associated bureaucracies and international systems. Local workers who understand the dominant culture, who know how the projects and international funding work, and who know how governments and communities operate will have the power to influence their own destiny and that of others. This need reflects the Wisdom face of informed learning.

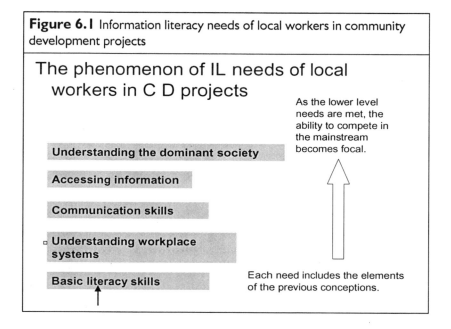

Figure 6.1 Information literacy needs of local workers in community development projects

In this research, development workers' views were of interest because, as a group, they are in a powerful position to ensure that the needs of local staff are met. Investigating development workers' views has given us an explicit picture of their perspectives and provided a framework for professional growth, discussion, debate, and training.

How do the different perceptions of information literacy needs reflect the GeST windows orientations? The need for basic literacy skills reflects the behavioral orientation, the Generic window. The workplace, communication, and sources needs reflect the sociocultural orientation, the Situated window, and the need to understand the dominant society reflects the critical orientation, the Transformative window. When, we as educators prepare students to engage in the workplace or community, we would want them to be able to adopt all three orientations.

Informed Learning in the Workplace

Just as students use information to learn in the academic context, so they will continue to use information to learn in the workplace. Informed learning, engaging in information practices to learn and adopting the most appropriate forms of information use in the process, is crucial to individual, team, and organizational learning. Learning organizations need informed learners. As with informed learning in the academic context, staff in workplaces are confronted with ongoing challenges in the technology sphere, large quantities of information of variable quality becoming available, and the need to draw upon their inner resources in dealing with problems and decisions. As I showed in chapter 5, such issues confront many professions in many industries.

As you read, consider a work team putting together a proposal for a new initiative, a senior executive confronted with substantial budget deficits, a team member reporting on annual objectives, and a new staff member creating client profiles. What might be the information practices they use? Planning, proposal writing, strategy development, project briefing, reporting? What might be the forms of information upon which they draw? Their own experiences, views of colleagues, data from a range of internal and external sources, media reports, government information, product information, patents, market research? How might their experiences of information use reflect the Seven Faces of Informed Learning? As we have seen in previous chapters, where creativity and physical engagement are vital to the information practice in question, the boundaries of what may be experienced as information widens.

What Does This Mean for Educating Informed Learners?
How can students be prepared for informed learning in the workplace? Quite apart from learning through discipline and professional information practices in their coursework, they also need to think through questions such as, *What does it take to be an informed learner in the workplace? What might be the features of organizations that support informed learning? What might the experience of informed learning in*

the workplace be like? We need to give students simulated experiences of the workplace, have them engage with the workplace through cooperative education, field work, industry projects, and other arrangements, or have them share and reflect on the workplace experiences that they may already have.

We should remember, when educating for informed learning in the workplace, to emphasize the social nature of using information to learn and the importance of working with intermediaries. Above all, we should remember that as information technology becomes increasingly seamless and user-friendly, the perennial need to make decisions and solve problems suggests that being able to work with information, communicate, and learn from each other continues to be of primary importance.

Kirk (2004, p. 197) suggests that students should be given the opportunity to appreciate how the experience of information use shapes judgment, decisions, and influence. If information can be transformative and information literacy can have an impact on social, economic, and cultural development, then curriculum design in some areas may be enhanced by a shift towards these directions.

What Does It Take to Be an Informed Learner in the Workplace?
Just like informed learning in the academic environment, informed learning in the workplace requires interdependence among colleagues and information and communication technologies appropriate to the needs of the group. How could students recognize characteristics of an organization that supports informed learning in the workplace? Using the broad lessons learned from investigating the Seven Faces of Informed Learning, we may infer that ensuring all participants in a workplace are empowered to use information to learn requires

- emphasis on the capacity to engage in broad professional responsibilities (information practices such as formulating strategy, problem identification, problem solving, decision making) rather than specific skills;
- social collaboration or interdependence between colleagues rather than emphasis on individual capability;
- partnership with information intermediaries;
- an emphasis on intellectual use of information rather than technical skills.

Peter Drucker (1992), almost 20 years ago, pointed to the need for organizations to become information literate. The questions that he suggested organizations should learn to ask ultimately must be considered by people. Such questions might include: *What information do we need in this organization? When do we need it? In what form? How do we get the information? What should we do with it?* At its core, the information-literate organization is a learning organization, a place where staff and organizational structures encourage continuous learning and ongoing renewal.

Being an informed learner in the workplace also requires reorienting ourselves to the broad range of forms which information might take. Tom Goad (2002) provides an extended discussion of information literacy in the workplace and identifies many forms and sources of information, such as body language, billboards, neon lights, signage, scrapbooks, libraries, art, policy, and customers, among others.

Table 6.4 Supporting informed learning in organizations (adapted from Bruce, 1999)

Seven Faces of Informed Learning	Organizational support for informed learning
Using technology to communicate and keep abreast of developments in the field	Environmental scanning and introduction of contemporary information technologies, enabling access to online information, both internal and external
Sourcing information to meet a learning need	E-library, corporate memory, availability of information intermediaries
Engaging in information processes to learn	Information processing, packaging of materials for internal and external consumption, access to professional development and networking opportunities
Making connections between information and learning needs	Information management processes
Knowledge construction	Building a corporate knowledge base, knowledge management
Knowledge extension	Research and development
Making wise use of information on behalf of others	Professional and corporate codes of ethics

What Might Be the Features of Organizations That Support Informed Learning?

Each of the Seven Faces is also associated with important workplace processes that link informed learning to the idea of learning organizations (Bruce, 1999). They suggest complementary organizational behaviors that need to be established to support the informed learning experience of individuals or work teams (See table 6.4).

The characteristics of an information-literate organization are explored by Carmel O'Sullivan (1999) in her description of an information-literate law firm. She proposes that to become and remain information literate, the following should be in place:

- Information produced by the organization and the knowledge of individuals should be captured and reused.
- The organization knows how it makes a profit and is able to use its structures and processes to maximize future profits.
- Staff understand what information and knowledge mean to the organization.
- The organization enables and encourages staff to do their job efficiently.
- The organization has information-literate staff that understand how information impacts their work and are able to find and use information as well as share their learning with other staff (pp. 177, 180).

Drawing from the Seven Faces of Informed Learning, we may pose a series of questions to determine whether the required organizational processes or infrastructures are in place:

- What environmental scanning and communication strategies are in place to ensure that staff stay up-to-date on important matters? (face 1)
- What resources and services are available to ensure that staff can access required information? (face 2)
- What are the organization's preferred approaches to problem solving, decision making, project management, and reporting? (face 3)
- What information-management strategies are in place? (face 4)
- Is the need for corporate memory taken seriously, and are processes established to help? (face 5)

- What research and development is encouraged? (face 6)
- What codes of ethics does the organization subscribe to? (face 7)

The importance of the information intermediary, knowledge manager, or librarian cannot be underestimated in the workplace experience of informed learning. For example, in chapter 3, I showed how professionals and academics from a wide range of disciplines wanted to engage in their own searching and also be able to engage the services of an intermediary in certain circumstances. The importance of the intermediary role is also highlighted in investigations of particular professional contexts. An ideal scenario for nurses, for example, has been described as involving a combination of independent information seeking and expert assistance. Such a combination is expected to result in both the effective use of time and quality-assured information provision (Farmer, Richardson, & Lawton, 1999).

What Might the Experience of Informed Learning in the Workplace Be Like?

The Seven Faces of Informed Learning were drawn from the research participants' experience of professional practice. Here I have adapted each of the Seven Faces to orient them more specifically toward the workplace experience of informed learning:

- *Information Awareness and Communication.* Members of a workplace are usually part of a work group or team. They use appropriate technologies to keep up-to-date with internal and external developments and to work with colleagues around the world. They belong to relevant professional forums and networks, making use of the communication systems used by that community.

- *Information Sources.* Members of a workplace have a range of information sources and spaces available to them. These may give them access to relevant scholarly, organizational, or social resources and point them towards ongoing conversations, events, or reports. The availability of information intermediaries is vital.

- *Information Processes.* Members of a workplace have established their personal preferences and strategies for working with information and with each other, for example, when problem solving and decision making. Information processes are creatively applied by different people in different circumstances.

- *Information Control.* Members of a workplace have an appreciation of the dimensions of their work that allow them to establish the relationships and connections between those things they recognize as information, including their ideas and reflections, and the projects they may be working on. People bring relevant information within their sphere of influence and organize it around projects being undertaken.
- *Knowledge Construction.* Members of a workplace understand their relevant professional bases and are able to think critically about emerging ideas and research outcomes. They have strategies for extending themselves into new areas.
- *Knowledge Extension.* Members of a workplace are aware of themselves and their engagement with others as catalysts of innovation and the development of new ideas or products.
- *Wisdom.* Members of a workplace are aware of the social implications of their work, of the need to make appropriate and wise use of information in the course of their work and in sharing their work with clients, colleagues, and the wider community.

Suggestions for Learning Design

Tom Goad (2002), in his book *Information Literacy and Workplace Performance*, provides an excellent and extensive discussion of many aspects of informed learning in the workplace. He focuses attention on several important information practices, decision making, problem solving, and strategic thinking, as well as suggesting many strategies for developing creativity.

More Suggestions for Learning Design

Sample tasks blending information interactions and content learning, with focus on community service and professional practice

Prepare a current-awareness strategy on the topic of creating, for example, environmentally friendly homes, and discuss what has been learned through implementation of that strategy over an eight-week period. A reflection might be included on what aspects of the strategy were useful and not useful, what resources were particularly useful, and how the strategy might be improved for the future. *This task, draws on a professional information practice. It introduces students to faces one and five of informed learning and uses the Learning to Learn, Social Impact, and Personal Relevance frames.*

Develop a package of materials for clients wanting to create, for example, an environmentally friendly home, and prepare a covering statement for the clients about how information has been gathered, the assessed quality of the information, and how that information might be put to use. *This task draws on a professional information practice. It introduces students to faces two, five, and seven of informed learning and uses the Learning to Learn and Social Impact frames.*

In your role as, for example, a community nurse or social worker, develop Web pages for a specified client group (e.g., young mothers or caregivers for the elderly). Include a statement about how the information was identified, the assessed quality of the information, and suggestions for how clients might use the information. Submit a report to the class or instructor indicating how you decided what material to use and not use and how to convey the content and other resources to users. *This task draws on a professional information practice. It introduces students to faces two, four, and seven of informed learning and uses the Learning to Learn and Social Impact frames.*

Informed Learning in the Community

Informed learning, vital to our academic and professional pursuits, has a pivotal role to play in our personal and community lives. In many of our everyday interests and concerns, we use information in order to learn.

As you read, imagine parents seeking information to help sick children; people with disabilities meeting their information needs online; bereaved adults sorting through the estate of a recently deceased relative; people from different cultural backgrounds attempting to solve legal problems; schoolchildren trying to make sense of information about drugs and drug abuse; citizens attempting to make sense of pre-election campaigning in print and in the broadcast media, as well as on YouTube and other emerging electronic spaces. How might their experience of information use reflect the Seven Faces of Informed Learning? What information practices might they use? What might be the forms of information upon which they draw?

The Prague Declaration, made by a group of international experts convened by UNESCO, the National Forum for Information Literacy

(NFIL), and the National Commission for Library and Information Science (NCLIS) identifies the "creation of an information society as key to social, cultural and economic development of individuals" (Thompson, 2003, p. 1). The declaration also identifies information literacy or informed learning, the ability to use information to learn, as a prerequisite for participating in an information society, as part of the basic human right of lifelong learning, and as an integral part of education for all.

For some, informed learning in the community may be about having a politically or financially savvy citizenry. It may also be about ensuring that people can use their recreation opportunities in ways that transform their lives for the better. Fundamentally, informed learning in the community must be about supporting and enriching communities, focusing on helping people use information to learn.

When we as educators concern ourselves with informed learning among our students, we also have the opportunity, through our educational endeavors, to bring informed learning into the community. This is most likely to be through the work our students do in such communities. Such community focus may also allow us to take a critical interest in those who are currently relatively disempowered in our global technological society, including women, children, and people with disabilities.

Joan Challinor (in Thompson, 2003), then chairperson of the U.S. National Commission for Library and Information Science, comments that "It is now past time to accept an 'information ... super-highway' on which men in the developed world, and some in the developing world, are traveling in fast cars while the majority of women in the developing world are walking barefoot on dirt-roads." She reminds us that our purpose in the informed learning agenda should be "to help the poorest help themselves to create richer and fuller lives that express and affirm their own distinctiveness in an increasingly interconnected global village" (pp. 24–25).

Suggestion for Learning Design

A useful Web site to browse for inspiration if you are interested in adopting a social justice focus belongs to the Association for Progressive Communications: Internet and ICTs for Social Justice and Development at http://www.apc.org (last accessed April 19, 2007).

What Does This Mean for Educating Informed Learners?
How can we prepare students for informed learning in the community? Quite apart from learning through discipline and professional information practices in their coursework, they also need to think through questions such as: *What does it take to be an informed learner in the community? What might be required to support informed learning? What might the experience of informed learning in the community be like?*

One way of understanding how different community groups might see their own experience of informed learning is to look at research into information literacy or information use in community settings. Below is one example of research of this kind.

The Online Information Practices of People With Disabilities
Christine Tilley's investigation (in Tilley, Bruce, Hallam, & Hills, 2006) of the information use of persons with disabilities reveals a very broad range of intense activity in the virtual environment. These uses are of considerable importance to disabled persons as they are engaging with information to enhance their quality of life. Being able to use technology, often through assistive technologies, and being able to use information to learn are essential in the range of domains that together form the virtual community space. Informed learning underpins the use of information in many of these domains.

The six types of e-communities within which information is used and informed learning occurs are listed below. For disabled persons reliant on the virtual environment, both information and technology skills are critical prerequisites for participation:

- *Education-oriented communities.* These include personal development and capacity building. They lead to higher levels of empowerment and participation in the community.
- *Fantasy-oriented communities.* These enable virtual reality activities where participants create environments, stories, and personalities and role-play.
- *Information-oriented communities.* These include information provision around health, travel, and accommodation, for example, in a context where social activities and interacting with information is strong.

- *Interest-oriented communities.* These include chat rooms, discussion groups, and message boards extensively used to focus on high-priority issues such as bioethics, disability rights, or moral purpose.
- *Relationship-oriented communities.* These include e-communities where building a personal community role, securing peer support, or bonding with others is key.
- *Transaction-oriented communities.* These include virtual communities where business transactions occur, such as banking, bill paying, stock-market trading, and teleworking.

One of the primary outcomes of this investigation was the identification of the need for "a sense of control" as the foundational element of virtual communities for the disabled. As they begin to engage with online communities, people with long-term disabilities regain a sense of control and independence in their lives through the use of technology. Such a sense of control requires the limiting of technological barriers and the enhancement of information and technology skills to make engagement with their critical information practices possible (Tilley et al., 2006).

If you are looking for research about how people interact with information in specific communities, many examples are available. Most of this research is unlikely to specifically examine the experience of using information to learn; however, it will provide descriptions of how people find or use information in particular contexts. *Library and Information Science Research* and *New Review of Information Behaviour* are two journals that may help. For example, Dunne (2002) explores information seeking and use by battered women, and Spink and Cole (2001) investigate the information-seeking channels used by African American low-income households.

Suggestions for Learning Design

How could Christine Tilley's investigation, described above, assist us in helping students become informed learners in the community? Clearly being part of an online learning community has substantial benefits in a whole range of ways for students who are differently abled. Being part of online learning communities would also bring substantial benefits to all students and perhaps help them become comfortable with becoming part of such communities in other parts of life.

The six orientations have implications for online learning communities. Students would be *seeking personal development* and capacity building. Virtual scenarios may present an element of *fantasy*. *Information* about their course of study and other issues would be required. Their *interest* levels would need to be fostered through chat rooms. *Relationships* would need to be established, and *transactions*, such as submitting assignments, would need to be made possible.

What Does It Take to Be an Informed Learner in the Community?

Just like informed learning in the academic and workplace environments, informed learning in the community requires interdependence among social networks and information and communication technologies appropriate to the needs of the group. Increasingly, community connectivity is happening via the Web. How could students recognize what is required to support informed learning in the community? How can they become aware of the freedoms offered and the constraints that continue to exist? Using the broad lessons learned from investigating the Seven Faces of Informed Learning, we may infer that ensuring members of a community are empowered to use information to learn requires

- an emphasis on the capacity to engage with broad community interests and responsibilities (information practices), rather than specific skills;
- collaboration or interdependence within social network, rather than emphasis on individual capability;
- the partnership of information intermediaries;
- an emphasis on intellectual use of information, rather than technical skills;
- an emphasis on the wise use of information.

Hilary Hughes, researching information use in the online environment, has been focusing on community issues. She writes (in Hughes, 2007) that life in the online world exposes us to a complex array of risks, responsibilities, and rights—security issues, ethical issues, freedom of information, and communication. Second Life, YouTube, and other forums are no longer just the domain of the young and savvy—more and more people of different demographics are exploring virtual worlds and Web 2.0. Increasingly, mainstream political and educational activities take place in cyberspace. Many groups use cyberspace for communication and advocacy.

These developments are accompanied by increasing discussion in the media about the dangers of Internet use: propaganda, cyberbullying, sexual exploitation, suicide pacts, and financial scams, among others. Behavioral solutions—banning, blocking, and filtering—tend to be counterproductive. In fact, they probably present enticing Net-savvy challenges.

Among all this bad press, information literacy seldom gets a mention. Yet it has the potential to enable people to freely and safely survive, learn, communicate, collaborate, create, and prosper in the online universe. Would it be more advantageous to promote individual and community learning that underpins the development of critical, ethical, and creative approaches to online information use—informed learning that enables us to recognize the risks, accept the responsibilities, and enjoy the rights of the online world?

What Does It Take to Support Informed Learning in the Community?
Supporting informed learning in the community involves making it possible for people to engage with information of all kinds in the various contexts for which they might need it. Such contexts might include health, education, finance, travel, entertainment, and career development.

Support is also required in the form of infrastructure: the carriers of information, such as books, cables, and computers and policy that encourages the provision of an information-rich environment. Government, educational institutions, libraries, and the nonprofit and corporate sectors all contribute. The provision of technology infrastructures is an inadequate response unless technology is only one part of a wider program that includes professional support, training, and education in working with information.

Support is required in the form of information professionals, especially librarians, employed to support people wherever engage in informed learning: in the workplace, universities, schools, the community, libraries and information centers, health centers, and sports complexes and other recreational spaces.

At present, governments and corporations invest millions of dollars on Internet security measures of various kinds. We could invest also in making people alert to their rights and responsibilities, as well as making it possible for them to enjoy and be supported in the use of digital environments. In a well-supported environment, people need never feel alone, disconnected, or incompetent.

What Might Informed Learning Look Like in Community Contexts?
Here I have adapted each of the Seven Faces to orient them towards the community experience of informed learning. In the following, the names of the Seven Faces have been modified to resonate better with the community context.

- *IT for a Purpose*

In our everyday lives, we use technology for a wide range of interactions. Our focus here is on using technology for communication and maintaining awareness about important aspects of the world around us. Computers, televisions, radios, and mobile devices all have their place. Communication and awareness not only are indicators of communities, they are also necessary for building communities. The social character of information literacy is critical to this experience. For example, people have used technology to form "giving circles" in which people give away and receive unwanted possessions, to renew and maintain friendships, and to record their life experience for sharing with others. New technology is often dealt with through sharing expertise; an individual may be a community expert or may be dependent on "service," assistance from distributors, friends, or relatives.

- *Sourcing Information*

In our everyday lives, working alone or in groups, with or without the support of information professionals, we spend much of our time sourcing useful information about areas of interest. Our focus here is on finding out about important stuff that is needed for a specific purpose, for example, around schools, the job market, political parties, world events, hobbies, travel information, or home services.

- *Problem Solving*

In our everyday lives, problem solving is a regular occurrence. Working with information in the problem-solving process requires understanding what works best for us in our circumstances. The focus here is on working out solutions and on identifying ways of doing things that work for me, or for my group, in our context. Do I start with the Internet? Do I start with a phone call? What steps will work for me? Developing the family tree, creating a financial strategy, planning educational futures, and tackling an unexpected health concern are only a few examples.

- *Getting Organized*

In our everyday lives, managing the ever-increasing range of resources around us is an imperative. Our focus here is on making connections or linkages around home projects. We need to understand how best to organize ourselves and our responsibilities. People need to consider personal and home records, financial records, entertainment, photography, video, Web pages, computer file structures, e-mail, their Web favorites, and the data in iPods and mobile phones.

- *Getting Informed*

In our everyday lives, we need to be able to learn about those things that are important to us when we want or need to explore unfamiliar territory. Some examples might be politics, health, finance, legal issues, or perhaps recreational concerns, rock climbing, netball, athletics, needlework, gardening, musical instrument making, or relaxation techniques. Our focus here is on understanding different perspectives and on finding our own way. We need to be able to critique the resources we use for learning, understanding their intended audience and the purposes of the authors or designers, or understanding the drivers, the motivations, and the passions of significant others from whom we may choose to learn.

- *Innovating*

In our everyday lives, we may design and make new things or develop creative solutions. We may tell stories or create music or art. We may establish new ways of handling our relationships. Our focus here is on using our intuition. We draw on our internal resources to move forward as best we can under many different circumstances.

- *Applying Wisdom*

In our everyday lives, we may choose to use information for the benefit of others. Our focus is on the "other" person or group in our purchasing, in our cooking, in the raising of our children, in our voting, or in our conversation. For example, we may choose, based on our own life experiences or values, to send our children to a particular school or to educate them at home; we may choose to purchase products from large retailers, from smaller businesses, or directly from the producer. We may choose to share and use what we know to benefit others as best we can.

How Could Students Use the Principles of Informed Learning in Communicating with Clients in the Community or Workplace?

When communicating with workplace colleagues or clients, it can be helpful for students to consider how the principles of informed learning may apply to helping others learn from them. What information may colleagues or clients be considering important—or be willing to accept as important? What could they be experiencing as information? What could be brought to their attention that they have not previously considered? What forms of information practice are colleagues or clients likely to be engaging in? How might it be possible to present a range of options and draw attention to key focal elements in each case?

This requires an important shift for students in thinking about themselves as learners and information users to recognizing others as learners and information users, as well as considering how seeing others that way might lead to new and interesting communication strategies.

Key Questions Arising From This Chapter—What Can We as Educators Do to Take This Agenda Further?

Informed Learning and Your Philosophy of Teaching

- Are community and workplace learning important to you, as a teacher?
- Which of the GeST windows resonates most with your practice? How might use of the other windows enhance your students' learning?
- What value can be brought to your students by engaging them with the community or workplace?
- How do you use information to learn in workplace or community contexts?

Informed Learning and Your Students

- What are your students' present experiences of informed learning in the workplace?
- What are your students' present experiences of informed learning in the community?
- How could you stretch their understandings, perhaps through inviting them to consider the experience of others?

Informed Learning and Your Curriculum Practice
- How does your present curriculum invite students into community and workplace experiences?
- How might you enhance your curriculum further?

Informed Learning in Your Field
- What opportunities does the character of your field provide for exploring workplace and community learning?

References

Bruce, C. S. (1999). Workplace experiences of information literacy. *International Journal of Information Management, 19*(1), 33–48.

Bruce, C. S. (2002). Information literacy as a catalyst for educational change: A background paper. White Paper prepared for UNESCO, the U.S. National Commission on Libraries and Information Science, and the National Forum on Information Literacy, for use at the Information Literacy, Meetings of Experts, Prague, The Czech Republic, September 2003 (pp. 1–17). [Retrieved October 7, 2006 from http://www.nclis.gov/libinter/infolitconf&meet/papers/bruce-fullpaper.pdf]

Drucker, P. (1992, Dec. 3). Be data literate … Know what to know. *The Wall Street Journal*, 16.

Dunne, J. (2002). Information seeking and use by battered women: A person-in-progressive-situations approach. *Library and Information Science Research, 24,* 343–355.

Farmer, J., Richardson, A., & Lawton, S. (1999). Improving access to information for nursing staff in remote areas: The potential of the Internet and other networked information sources. *International Journal of Information Management, 19*(1), 49–62.

Goad, T. (2002). *Information literacy and workplace performance*. Westport, CT: Quorum Books.

Hughes, H. (2007). Risks, responsibilities and rights of life online (personal correspondence, August 31, 2007).

Lupton, M., & Bruce, C. (manuscript). Windows on information literacy worlds: The GeST model.

McMahon, C., & Bruce, C. (2002). Information literacy needs of local staff in cross-cultural development projects. *International Journal of Community Development, 14,* 113–127.

Minahan, S., & Cox., J. (2007). Stich'n'bitch cyberfeminism, a third place and the new materiality. *Journal of Material Culture, 12*(1), 5–21.

O'Sullivan, C. (1999). Profiling an information literate law firm. In D. Booker (Ed.), *Concept, challenge and conundrum: From library skills to informa-*

tion literacy. *Proceedings of the fourth national information literacy confer-
ence conducted by the University of South Australia Library and the ALIA
Information Literacy Special Interest Group, Adelaide, University of South
Australia Library*, pp. 176–181.

Spink, A., & Cole, C. (2001). Information and poverty: Information seeking
channels used by African American low income households. *Library and
Information Science Research, 23*, 45–65.

Thompson, S. (2003). The Prague declaration, U.S. Commission on Libraries
and Information Science, December 2003. Available at: http://www.nclis.
gov/libinter/infolitconf&meet/post-infolitconf&meet/FinalReportPrague.
pdf (accessed: April 20, 2007).

Tilley, C., Bruce, C., Hallam, G., & Hills, A. (2006). A model for the development of virtual communities for people with long-term, severe, physical
disabilities. *Information Research, 11*(3), April 2006.

Chapter 7

Informed Learning in the Research Community

Opening Narrative

Academic research is another form of learning with which Jane and Steve might be involved. It is a complex information practice in its own right. In working with their research students, and in their own research work, Steve and Jane encounter many different views around questions such as: What kinds of projects are appropriate, or not appropriate, to pursue? What information do we need to gather to get started and to delve deeper? Where, or from whom, should we seek information? What lines should we pursue or discard? All of these are information-based decisions, reflecting the character of research as a site of information practice. Why do people hold such diverse views in response to such questions? Jane and Steve may be helped by considering the diverse views held by their students and colleagues of the research territory they work within.

In working with their colleagues, Jane and Steve notice that there are many views of research, just as there are many views of learning, and there are many information practices involved in the many facets of the research process. What might informed learning look like in the research context?

In this chapter, I explore the idea of informed learning in the research community and its applicability to research higher-degree study and supervision. It mirrors the early chapters' examination of what we know about ways of seeing learning and information use by exploring recent developments in uncovering the experience of research, examining the notion of Six Frames for Informed Learning in the context of learning to research, and adapting the Seven Faces of Informed Learning to the research setting. Some suggestions are made about possible relationships between information use and research. In this chapter, I focus primarily on researchers and what we know of academic experiences in that role; in the next chapter, I focus on the experience of research students.

What Do We Know About the Experience of Research?

Understanding the research experience helps us to bring research students and early career researchers into appropriate experiences. At present, we know a little about researchers' and research students' experiences of research. We know less about the relationship between the experience of information use and research outcomes.

Like learning and information literacy, research and learning to research are experienced differently in the community of researchers. Supervisors or advisers of research students with an interest in supervision as a teaching–learning practice can use insights into those experiences, in the same way that teachers of undergraduate students use insights into different experiences of learning.

The most influential and substantial investigation into researchers' varying experiences of research was conducted by Angela Brew (2001), who describes four variations in the experience of research. In her *domino conception,* research is seen as separate tasks or events that impact on one another. These individual separate elements are the focus of researchers' attention and need to be synthesized as part of the research process. In her *trading conception,* research is seen as a social phenomenon, with focus on research products such as publications and grants. In her *layer conception,* researchers focus on their data and on discovering the meanings embedded there. In her *journey conception,* researchers focus on themselves as researchers and the influence of their research on themselves and society.

A meta-analysis of academics' research experiences proposes that the research experience may be described in terms of four foci (Akerlind, 2008): (a) research intention: who is affected by the research, (b) research outcomes: the anticipated impact of the research, (c) research questions: the nature of the object of study, and (d) research process: how research is undertaken. Gerlese Akerlind also shows how, using this framework, research may be said to be experienced in four different ways: as fulfilling academic requirements, as a personal achievement, as a route to personal understanding, or as impetus for change to benefit a larger community.

Research supervisors' or advisers' views of research have been identified as being technical, applying systematic techniques; creative and innovative; integrating complexity; synthesizing complex data or knowledge; or bringing about new ways of seeing (Kiley & Mullins, 2005).

Six Frames for Informed Learning and the Higher-Degree Research Experience

As research supervisors adopt the role of teacher or learning facilitator, their views of information use and information practices may influence the learning-to-research process along the lines suggested by the Six Frames for Informed Learning (chapter 2). Given our emerging insights into the experience of research, is it possible to adapt the Six Frames for Informed Learning to the higher-degree research experience? Is it conceivable, for example, that supervisors may at some times adopt a Content frame, both substantively and methodologically, and at other times may adopt a Competency frame—or the Learning to Learn, Personal Relevance, Social Impact, or Relational frames? Certainly, different supervisors and different stakeholders in the research higher-degree environment have different views and approaches to research and learning to research.

Using the insights we have available from Wood (2006), Brew (2001), Kiley and Mullins (2005), and Meyer, Shanahan, and Laugksch (2005), I have developed a *learning to research*–oriented version of the Six Frames for Informed Learning (see table 7.1). These frames bring students', researchers', and supervisors' views of research and learning to research together with the Six Frames for Informed Learning. They provide broad curriculum orientations for the learning-to-research context and associate different ways of thinking about information use with the different orientations. As we consider supervision as a site of teaching and learning practice, the different frames can be used to expand or enhance that experience.

The Content Frame

In the Content frame, learning to research is seen as becoming an expert in the content area, and research is seen as being about increasing knowledge or discovering truth. In this frame, information may be seen as external, having independent existence and requiring discovery. Using information may be seen as applying knowledge about the world of information and about how information is created in the discipline.

The Competency Frame

In the Competency frame, learning to research is seen as learning research techniques, and research is seen as a series of tasks, information

Table 7.1 Six Frames for Informed Learning adapted for the higher-degree research context

Frame	Learning to research is seen as ...	Research is seen as ...	Information (in the research context) is seen as ...	Information use is experienced as ...
Content	becoming expert in the content area	increasing knowledge, discovering truth	external, having an independent existence requiring discovery	applying knowledge about the world of information and about how information is created in the discipline
Competency	learning research techniques	a series of tasks, applying systematic techniques, gathering information	external, having an independent existence requiring discovery	implementing skills and techniques
Learning to Learn	learning to make meaning, discover, solve problems, create new ideas	seeking meaning or integrating complexity, synthesizing complex data or knowledge, an insightful process, finding solutions to problems	internal, subjective, constructed by researchers	an integral part of the research process
Personal Relevance	coming to understand the location of self in the research process	a journey influencing self, changing as a person, a route to personal understanding	that which informs me and my research journey	using information for personal and research benefit
Social Impact	coming to understand the impact of research on society	a journey benefiting society or the profession, trading to secure desired outcomes	socially derived and situated	using information and knowledge to secure social futures
Relational	coming to see research as discovering new views of the research object, or territory	coming to see differently	objective, subjective or transformative	working with the complex of different ways of using information

gathering, or the application of systematic techniques. In this frame, information may also be seen as external, having independent existence and requiring discovery. Information use may be seen as making use of a set of skills and techniques.

The Learning to Learn Frame

In the Learning to Learn frame, learning to research is seen as learning to make meaning, discover, solve problems, and create new ideas, and research is seen as seeking meaning, synthesizing complex data or knowledge, or finding solutions to problems. In this frame, information is seen as subjective and constructed by researchers. Information use is seen as an integral part of the research process.

The Personal Relevance frame

In the Personal Relevance frame, learning to research is coming to understand one's own place in the research process, and research is seen as a journey that benefits society and the professions. In this frame, information is that which informs the researcher and his or her research journey. Information use is conducting research for personal and community benefit.

The Social Impact Frame

In the Social Impact frame, learning to research is seen as coming to understand the impact of research upon society, and research is seen to be a journey benefiting society. In this frame, information is socially derived or situated. Information use is seen as using information and knowledge to secure social futures.

The Relational Frame

In the Relational frame, learning to research is coming to see research as discovering new views of the research object or territories, and research is about learning at the collective level, where communities of experts progressively come to see differently those things that they are researching (Bowden & Marton, 1998). Information use is seen as working with the complex of different ways of using information.

Using the Six Frames in the Higher-Degree Research Context

The research frames for informed learning can also be used to better understand our context, or to bring about innovation.

The frames provide a basis from which to understand the different perspectives of colleagues, students, and other stakeholders. It is likely that different stakeholders will adopt different frames, and also that students may not always adopt the same frames as their supervisors. The frames allow us to ask questions about the experiences our students currently have, the experiences we wish them to engage with, and how we might bring that about. They can also be used to challenge us, as supervisors, to adopt alternative orientations with our students.

Researchers as Informed Learners

In researching the Seven Faces of Informed Learning, many of the participants were researchers. How could that model of using information to learn assist us in understanding the information use processes of researchers? Looking at each face, we can establish connections with well-established information-use processes in the research community, for example:

- *Information Awareness and Communication.* Researchers are usually members of a research community, well-established in relevant research forums and networks, making use of the communication systems used by that community.

- *Information Sources.* Researchers are familiar with the range of information sources and spaces that give them access to relevant scholarly, organizational, or social conversations, events, or reports.

- *Information Processes.* Researchers have established their personal preferences and strategies for working with information.

- *Information Control.* Researchers have an appreciation of the dimensions of their work that allow them to establish the relationships and connections between various information artifacts or ideas and their evolving contributions.

- *Knowledge Construction.* Researchers understand their relevant research bases and are able to think critically about the disciplines and territories that are bound up with their research intentions and processes. They have strategies for extending themselves into new areas.

- *Knowledge Extension.* Researchers are aware of themselves and their engagement with others as catalysts of innovation and the development of new ideas or products.

- *Wisdom.* Researchers need to be aware of the social implications of their work, of the need to make appropriate and wise use of information in the course of their research and in their communication of their work to research peers as well as to the wider community.

On the Relationship Between Information Use and Research

In the undergraduate experience of learning, we have a number of investigations that have directly explored aspects of the relationship between learning and information use (see chapter 4). In the research space, we do not have similar investigations. There are, however, some inferences that can be drawn from existing research. I propose some possible relationships below.

The Inseparable Nature of Information Use and Research

In the research environment, information use is unlikely to be seen by experienced researchers as a "separable" process; rather, it is closely entwined with the research process. It is one of the essential ingredients that makes discovery, personal growth, or social change possible. Consider, for example, the way in which a researcher chooses to make use of an information artifact—a document, work of art, Web page, blog, or podcast. Stoan (1991) suggests that researchers bestow relevance on documents by thinking about them in ways that enable the documents to fit into the researchers' developing research schemes. We could say that there is an interaction between the information artifact and the research scheme that is mediated by the mind of the researcher. Similarly, Park (1993) suggests more explicitly that researchers are "continuously assessing the value of information and interpreting a citation in order to learn and shape the research problem." As supervisors, we need to remain open to the possibility that research candidates may adopt sequential approaches to information use, of the kind identified by Lupton (2008, see chapter 4), and we need to consider how we would wish to influence our students in this area.

Researchers' Interpretation of Their Research Territory May Influence How They Use and Engage With Information

How researchers see their research field is a context for information use, just as their perception of an information practice, such as literature reviews, forms such a context. Researchers' view of what does or does not constitute their field is likely to influence

- what information they might see, or be willing to see;
- how they interact with that information;
- how they judge its relevance;
- how they judge or otherwise use the information;
- the character of the new information or knowledge that they generate.

Simple informational decisions that potentially have far-reaching influences on research are governed by broader ways of seeing the world. In order to be empowered to choose, people need to be aware of the different ways of seeing available within their research community.

An example of the way in which researchers may see their research object or territories is found in an investigation of information technology (IT) researchers' different ways of experiencing IT research (Pham, Bruce & Stoodley, 2005). Altogether, eight ways of seeing IT research were found, each of which constructed the research object and territory in different ways:

- *The technology conception.* IT research is seen as research that is directed towards technology and includes the manufacturing of technological artifacts, the development of new systems, or the creation of code. The historical roots of IT, its foundations in engineering mathematics and machine learning, for example, influence the character of the field. Researchers are focused on technology, and the territory is delimited by interest in those artifacts that are used in the information environment: routers, switches, computers, and mobile devices. Application of technology such as medical information systems would not be included in the scope of the field.

- *The information conception.* IT research is seen as research that is directed towards information processing, including security, organization, and storage of information. Researchers are focused on information, with technology in the background, seen as a tool for manipulating information. The use to which technology is put, information processing, delimits the research territory. In this view, concerns about the content of information appear outside the scope of the field.

- *The information and technology conception.* IT research is seen as research that is directed towards both information and technology, including activities such as information collection, information provision, and information security. Researchers are focused on both information and technology simultaneously. The convergence of information and IT is integral to the formation of the field. The research territory spans that of both the information and technology conceptions above. Research into information or technology in isolation from the other is not considered to be IT research.

- *The communication conception.* IT research is seen as research directed towards the experience of communication among people, including the development of information exchange strategies, methods of information transfer, facilitation of thinking, and learning support. Researchers are focused simultaneously on information, technology, and people, a focus that finds expression in an interest in communication. In this way of seeing, the web of relationships between people, technology, information, and the impact of IT on people extends the territory of IT.

- *The ubiquitous conception.* IT research is seen as research directed towards the application of technology to all human endeavor; all aspects of developing, implementing, and maintaining systems are part of the field, as is the application of IT methodology to other disciplines. Researchers are focused on the application and use of IT in any setting; consequently, the territory of IT research is unbounded.

- *The sanctioned, constructed, and dialectic conceptions.* IT research is seen as constructed, not by the artifacts and the implementation, but by people. In the sanctioned conception, the field of IT research is determined by expert others; in the constructed conception, the field is determined by researchers actively engaged in IT research; in the dialectic conception, the field is negotiated by the goals of an individual researcher and expert gatekeepers of the field.

All the views together form the field of IT research. Nevertheless, individual researchers adopt different ways of seeing for different purposes and in different contexts. Each view is unique and will lead to different informational worlds being seen as relevant. For example, researchers adopting a technology conception may not interact with the information literature, and similarly, researchers adopting an information conception may not interact with the technology literature. Researchers adopting an information and technology conception are more likely to interact with the literature of both areas. Again, these are issues worth being mindful of as we work with our research candidates in our fields.

Researchers' Views of Information May Be Related to Their Conceptions of Significance and Value in Research

How researchers regard information and how they judge its relevance may be related to their ways of seeing the significance and value of research. Bruce, Pham, and Stoodley (2004) asked information technology researchers from different subdisciplines about how they decided whether the projects they reported in a series of research papers were significant or valuable or not. The responses of these researchers give us some glimpses into researchers as information users and how they may judge the quality or relevance of research information. Altogether, there were four different ways discovered of attributing significance and value to research projects:

• *Significance and value are experienced as contributing to personal goals.* Here, the researchers' focus is on professional interest or professional gain: Will the project contribute to my teaching or my career? Alternatively, they may be fundamentally interested because their curiosity is aroused. Researchers experiencing significance and value this way may approach information and information use with similar criteria in mind.

• *Significance and value are experienced as contributing to the research economy.* Here, the researchers' focus is on the currencies of research: Will the project lead to promotion, funding, or employment for members of the team? These are not personal issues, but rather consideration to take into account for the broader research team. For researchers experiencing significance and value this way, valuable information will also be that which contributes to the evolution of the research group.

• *Significance and value are experienced as contributing to research project design.* Here, the researchers' focus is on project design: Is the project methodologically sound? Is it rigorous and valid? Is it creative? For researchers experiencing significance and value this way, valuable information will contribute to an understanding of methodological advances and interpretation.

• *Significance and value are experienced as contributing to the end users of the research outcomes.* Here, the researchers' focus is on the social impact of research, particularly any consequences for people and social subgroups: Will the project improve current practices? Will it have a constructive influence on the world? Researchers experiencing significance and value this way are likely to see valuable information as that which will have an impact or enable them to contribute to such positive outcomes.

The Diverse Forms of Information in the Research Context

The question of what forms information may take in research should also remain open. In thinking about using information for research, we need to consider research data, previously documented research, people, organizations, art, the environment, political campaigns, the deliberations of scholars, and the conversations of everyday life. The questions of what constitutes information and the different ways in which information is experienced in research, if subject to reflection, may suggest useful paths for ourselves as researchers as well as for researchers in training. Undoubtedly, information would be constituted differently and would appear in different forms in different disciplines and subdisciplines.

Key Questions Arising From This Chapter—What Can We as Educators Do to Take This Agenda Further?

In research, there are many purposes for which information might be used and many forms that information might take, most of which are presently under-researched.

Informed Learning and Your Philosophy of Research Supervision
- How do you see research and learning to research?
- Which frames for informed learning best resonate with your supervisory practice?
- What relationships can you see between your views of research and your preferred frames for informed learning?
- What are your views of your research object or research territory?

Informed Learning and Your Research Students
- What are your students' views of research and learning to research?
- Which frames for informed learning might your research students be adopting?

Informed Learning and Your Supervisory Practice
- Which frames for informed learning are presently dominating your practice?
- How might your supervisory practice change if you adopted alternative frames?
- Describe your present practice and proposed future practice.
- Identify something that your students are learning to research, and consider what their experience might look like through each of the different frames.

Informed Learning and Research in Your Field
- How do you use information as a researcher?
- What are the important forms of information in your research field?
- What are the important information practices in your research field?
- Which frames for informed learning best reflect supervisory practice or the pedagogy of supervision in your field or discipline?
- How could the other frames contribute?
- How do researchers in your community see their research object and territory? How does this influence what they consider to be relevant information?

References

Akerlind, G. (2008). An academic perspective on research and being a researcher: An integration of the literature, *Studies in Higher Education, 33*(1), 17-31.

Bowden, J., & Marton, F. (1998). *The university of learning: Beyond quality and competence in higher education.* London: Kogan Page.

Brew, A. (2001). Conceptions of research: A phenomenographic study. *Studies in Higher Education, 26*(3), 271–285.

Bruce, C., Pham, B., & Stoodley, I. (2004). Constituting the significance and value of research: Views from information technology academics and industry professionals. *Studies in Higher Education, 29*(2), 219–239.

Kiley, M., & Mullins, G. (2005). Supervisors' conceptions of research: What are they? *Scandinavian Journal of Educational Research, 49,* 245–262.

Lupton, M. (2008) *Information literacy and learning.* PhD thesis. Brisbane, Australia: Queensland University of Technology. (Available at http://adt.library.qut.edu.au)

Meyer, J., Shanahan, M., & Laugksch, R. (2005). Students' conceptions of research. I: A qualitative and quantitative analysis. *Scandinavian Journal of Educational Research, 49,* 225–244.

Pham, B., Bruce, C., & Stoodley, I. (2005). Constituting information technology research: The experience of IT researchers. *Higher Education Research and Development, 24*(3), 215–232.

Park, T. K. (1993). The nature of relevance in information retrieval: An empirical study. *Library Quarterly, 63,* 318–51.

Stoan, S. S. (1991). Research and information retrieval among academic researchers: Implications for library instruction. *Library Trends, 39*(3), 238–57.

Wood, K. (2006). Changing as a person: The experience of learning to research in the social sciences. *Higher Education Research and Development, 25*(1), 53–66.

Chapter 8

Research Higher-Degree Students and Informed Learning

Opening Narrative

Jane and Steve have been in the university for a few years now, and their role as research supervisors is starting to expand. They are finding that working with research students and the need to help the students establish themselves as independent learners is influencing their undergraduate learning design. As students who have had a focus on information use in their undergraduate years come to Jane and Steve for honors and research higher-degree work, they find that these students are better prepared for the research environment. Steve and Jane recognize the need to further embed research skills in their undergraduate curriculum.

The cultural, academic, and professional background of research students is no less diverse than that of the undergraduate population. Steve and Jane believe that if information practices are important in undergraduate education, it would make sense that they should be a focus for research higher-degree students and their supervisors as well. While there are many information practices associated with the research higher degree, they discover that one such practice, the preparation of a literature review, has already received considerable attention from the relational perspective. In work with their students, they are able to use the insights and strategies arising from the available picture of students' diverse ways of experiencing the literature review.

Steve and Jane are surprised to find how diverse the different ways of experiencing the literature review are. It appears that their role as supervisors is to make students aware of this diversity and shepherd them into adopting the relevant perspective at different stages of the process. As with their other experiences of information literacy education, they find that the relational model informs them about the focus that students need to adopt in order to appropriate a particular perspective.

In this chapter, I explore informed learning in the research higher-degree context. It opens with an overview of how research is experienced by students. The idea of informed learning itself is envisioned from a

146

research student's perspective, followed by an exploration of the literature review as an example of an information practice seen in different
ways by research students. Different ways of experiencing the literature
review itself and the scope of the literature review are described. Reflective strategies for expanding students' experience are suggested.

Informed Learning Draws From Our Understanding of the Experience of Learning to Research

Our understanding of variation in the experience of learning and teaching, or of supervision, in the higher-degree research context is not as
extensive as our understanding of undergraduate learning. As with
the undergraduate learning experience, we can expect that working
with information effectively as a researcher occurs in a context where
students, supervisors, and other researchers have different ways of
seeing or experiencing important aspects of that environment. Just as
undergraduate learners experience learning differently, research students
experience research differently. While this is in some ways self-evident,
there is only an embryonic research base to support the notion. This
research, based on content analysis, indicates that postgraduate students
learning to research, in this case predominantly women in South Africa
and Australia, may see research as

- the gathering of information, including the collection of data
  for analysis;
- discovering truth, seeking out the truth or establishing the
  truth about something;
- an insightful process, deepening or extending our
  understanding of existing knowledge;
- re-search, returning to previous research and making new
  findings;
- finding solutions to problems, or answering questions (Meyer,
  Shanahan, & Laugksch, 2005).

There is also an emerging view that research students in the education discipline, particularly women, experience learning to research as
changing as a person. Several dimensions of changing as a person have
been identified as: recognizing alternative epistemological stances, seeking to understand the basis of others' perspectives, realizing differences
in the fundamental nature of learning, engaging in personal reflection

and appreciating its role in interpretation and understanding, and realizing differences in the nature of professional practice (Wood, 2006).

Helping Research Students Is About Understanding Their Experience of Informed Learning

One of the purposes of the research higher degree is to bring neophyte researchers into significant communities of practice in their field and to enable them to experience research and information use in the research process as their more experienced counterparts might do. As supervisors, it is our responsibility to enhance students' existing experience and usher them into other experiences that we may consider desirable.

What experiences of informed learning can we expect research students to be engaging with, perhaps from the earliest stages of their candidature? I have adapted the Seven Faces of Informed Learning and identified what they may mean for research students as follows:

• *Information Awareness and Communication.* Research students are situating themselves in the community of researchers, establishing themselves in relevant research forums and networks, and making use of the communication systems used by that community.

• *Information Sources.* Research students are becoming familiar with the range of information sources and spaces available to them, which give them access to relevant resources: scholarly, organizational, or social; conversations, events, or reports.

• *Information Processes.* Research students are enhancing their personal preferences and strategies for working with information.

• *Information Control.* Research students are gaining an increasing appreciation of the dimensions of their work in order to establish the relationships and connections between various information artifacts or ideas and their emerging position.

• *Knowledge Construction.* Research students need to understand their relevant research bases and be able to think critically about the disciplines and territories that are bound up with their research intentions and processes.

• *Knowledge Extension.* Research students need to be aware of themselves and their engagement with others as catalysts of innovation and the development of new ideas or products.

• *Wisdom.* Research students need to be aware of the social implications of their work, of the need to make appropriate and wise use of information in the course of their research and in their communication of their work to research peers as well as to the wider community.

Information use, as described above, comprises a broad set of processes or orientations that are implemented or adopted in many information practices. Researchers from all disciplines engage with a range of information practices that are likely to need developing and polishing as research students embark on their journey of learning to research. Some such practices may include archival research, grant writing, journal article writing, thesis writing, the development of research methods or techniques, reviewing, and sourcing examples of research impact, among others. These practices would be important to research students in prospective research-based employment, whether this be with commercial, government, or university research groups.

In the next section, I look at one of these information practices through the Relational frame, examining research students' experiences of reviewing the literature.

Research Students' Experiences of the Literature Review

From the Relational perspective, insights are available into critical differences in research students' ways of experiencing their literature review (Bruce, 1994). While not all disciplines require extensive engagement with the literature, most technical, scientific, and social science disciplines expect interaction with the literature as a demonstration of professional proficiency.

What is required to help higher-degree research students interact with the literature and write literature reviews? Like the wider research process itself, the literature review is an information practice within which the various information-use processes are implemented—staying informed, seeking for sources, controlling information, using personal processes, constructing knowledge, innovating, and using information wisely. The literature review as an information practice, however, may also be experienced differently, and students need to develop an understanding of the various forms of experiencing such practices as part of the process of becoming researchers. In the case of the literature review, seven different ways of experiencing have been identified:

- *Literature review as a list.* In this conception, the literature review is experienced as a list or collection of items representing the literature of the area of study. Students' focus is on discrete items, such as conference papers, journal articles, books, newspapers, creative works, and patents. The list may take the form of an annotated bibliography, including elements of a citation; a description of each item, which may be critical or not; relevant keywords; and important sources (journals, conferences, Web sites). Students experiencing the literature review this way may talk about it as a "a list of relevant articles," "a comprehensive list," or "concise summaries."

- *Literature review as a search.* In this conception, the literature review is experienced as a process of identifying information or literature relevant to the area of study. Students focus on the act of finding or looking for resources, which may involve going through a source such as a database or a key article to identify useful information. Students experiencing the literature review this way may talk about it as "an exploration of relevant materials for relevant materials," "involving the use of multiple search techniques," or "finding relevant and up-to-date information."

- *Literature review as a survey.* In this conception, the literature review is experienced as an investigation of past and present writing or research in one or more areas of interest. Students' focus is on the literature, the knowledge base or discourse of the discipline, including research methodologies. The investigation of the literature may be active, critical, and analytical; or passive, noncritical, and descriptive. Students experiencing the literature review this way may talk about it as "a look across past and current information," "examining current knowledge in the field," or "a critical appraisal."

- *Literature review as a vehicle for learning.* In this conception, the literature review is experienced as having an impact on the researcher. Students' focus is on themselves as researchers and on their developing knowledge or understanding. There is likely to be an element of using the literature review as a sounding board for checking ideas or testing personal perceptions. Students experiencing the literature review this way may talk about it as "checking our own observations," "broadening our concepts," or "understanding the dimensions of a subject."

- *Literature review as a research facilitator.* In this conception, the literature review is experienced as relating specifically to the research that is being, or about to be, undertaken. It may support, influence, direct, shape, or change the research. Students' focus is on their work at various stages, from identifying a topic, supporting a methodology, and providing a context, to changing the direction of the research. Students experiencing the literature review this way may talk about it as "a dynamic process with feedback into the research project," "changing many of the researcher's original ideas and plans," "part and parcel of the thought process to achieve the goal of the study," or "the backbone of the research and ongoing throughout."

• *Literature review as a report.* In this conception, the literature review is experienced as a written discussion of literature, drawing on investigations previously undertaken. Students' focus is on framing a written discourse about the literature, which may be established as a component part of the thesis or research report. Students experiencing the literature review this way may talk about it as "a daunting writing process" or " a report on areas of literature."

Helping Your Research Students

- What language are you and your students using as you talk about their literature reviews?
- What ways of experiencing their reviews are those conversations pointing toward?
- What experiences would you wish your students to adopt at that point of their candidature?
- How can you orient your students towards the preferred experiences?

Research Students' Experience of Scoping Their Literature Review

How do research students decide where to draw the boundaries when they are reviewing the literature? What should they attend to, or not attend to, as they discover new worlds impinging on their areas of interest? Research students from a wide range of disciplines have been shown to focus on one or more of eight different issues as they consider the problem of scope (described later in this section): topicality, comprehensiveness, breadth, relevance, authority, availability, currency, and exclusion (Bruce, 2001). These ways of seeing the scope of their literature review may be grouped around two approaches:

- *The subjective approach to scope.* Here belong foci on breadth, relevance, authority, and exclusion. In the subjective approach, information is interpreted as subjective; relevance is established by the researcher in his or her interpretation of the documents or information artifacts; and evolving, changing relationships are established between the researcher and those documents.

- *The objective approach to scope.* Here belong the foci on topicality, comprehensiveness, availability, and timeliness. In the objective approach, information is interpreted as objective, and topical forms of relevance are preferred. Relevance is considered an attribute of the document rather than a relationship with the research project established by the researcher.

Subjective approaches are likely to be more beneficial to research students. Adopting different ways of thinking about information and relevance will make their engagement with literature reviews more manageable.

The eight foci influencing how students scope their literature review may be described as follows:

- *Topicality.* In this way of seeing, students focus on the topic or subject area of their research. It is the simplest view of the scope of the literature review. Students are recognizing that their literature review must be about something, some "topic," and believe that any resources included should be about that topic. The "topic" does not include general background or associated and supporting topics. This focus is a somewhat limiting approach to the literature review, as it does not recognize that literature or material in other areas could be of considerable interest to the research in progress. If your students are adopting this view, encourage them to consider not only the many facets of their area but also the possible contributions of other disciplines or associated fields.

- *Comprehensiveness.* In this way of seeing, students focus on the need to retrieve all possible materials in the area of their research. They are endeavoring to be exhaustive in their treatment. Concern for comprehensiveness holds a significant place in students' considerations of scope. It is sometimes linked with the other areas of focus. For example, a student seeking "the maximum amount of relevant and up-to-date information" links this focus with that of currency. A student seeking "All available relevant literature" links this focus with that of availability. Students adopting this view are likely to find it somewhat overwhelming. They need to be encouraged to relinquish their attempts to be comprehensive and attend instead to learning to discern significant and representative works. Students working in emerging areas who find little despite their insistence on being comprehensive will need to branch out into related fields.

- *Breadth.* In this way of seeing, students focus on writing beyond their specific topic or field of interest. They seek out background information, related disciplines, and supporting areas. The focus on breadth is not as ambitious as the focus on comprehensiveness, nor does it unduly confine students' areas of interest. It permits exploration beyond the confines of the specific and is more flexible than the focus on topicality. If your students are adopting this view, encourage them to understand the interrelationship between their different areas of interest and the relationship of those areas to their own area of study.

- *Relevance.* In this way of seeing, students focus on relevant materials. Relevance differs from topicality because literature may be considered relevant while not being in the area of study. For example, students researching peer tutoring may also be interested in the literature on mentoring. This focus more closely resembles in interest in psychological relevance than topical relevance. Students adopting this view are exploring different fields of interest and building potential relationships with their work. As relevance criteria are likely to change as a research project progresses, students would benefit from articulating these criteria.

- *Authority.* In this way of seeing, students focus on authoritative literature of fundamental importance to their research area. Like exclusion, this is a selective focus. An interest in authority requires students to be able to critically assess material and represents an important shift away from the need for comprehensiveness.

- *Availability.* In this way of seeing, students focus on whether they can easily source the literature. What they cannot easily source is likely to be put to one side. Many students are reluctant to seek out material that is not readily available, either electronically, from their personal contacts, or from easily accessible libraries. Costs and time delays may be barriers to students obtaining potentially valuable documents.

- *Currency.* In this way of seeing, students focus on the need for timely, or up-to-date, information. In this experience, historical material is not of interest for its own sake, and students are not always specific about the time span involved. Students adopting this view should be encouraged to review earlier resources and discuss how they are deciding what is and is not relevant to their own area of interest.

- *Exclusion.* In this way of seeing, students focus on the need to exclude particular fields or forms of information. This demonstrates a selective rather than a comprehensive approach to the literature. Although students concerned with relevance would need to make decisions about what is not relevant, this is not usually done explicitly. Students would benefit from being explicit about what will be excluded from their literature reviews.

Help Your Research Students by Exploring Together
- What language are you and your students using as you talk about the scope of their literature reviews?
- What ways of experiencing the scope of their review are those conversations pointing towards?
- What experiences would you wish your students to adopt at that point of their candidature?
- How can you orient your students towards the preferred experiences?

Research Students' Experiences of Using Controlled Vocabulary in Database Searching

In chapter 4, I reviewed some different ways in which students see Internet searching and identified the need for students to focus on both the structure of the information environment and the quality of the resources they gain access to in order to gain the maximum benefit from their Internet interactions for learning. Research students need to have an understanding of structured databases available via the Internet in order to access research literature.

In our contemporary online environment, researchers and research students need to understand the difference between computer-generated databases and those where human intervention provides a higher level of control for searchers. For example, if someone is using Web of Science for citation searching, no control of cited forms exists, and the searcher needs to identify all possible forms that the citation might take.

An important aspect of those structured databases with which research students need to interact is the controlled vocabularies that are designed to make it possible for searchers to dialogue meaningfully with the database. Klaus (2000) suggests that the process of interacting with research literature through a database may be likened to an "online dialogue" and that the controlled vocabulary used to connect similar items in the database represents a shared language used by both the database and the searcher.

If used appropriately by the database creator and users, the controlled vocabulary will ensure, for example, that a researcher looking for material about environmental disasters will find relevant resources, even if the phrase *environmental disaster* is not used anywhere in the text of the articles in that database. Similarly, the researcher may use the controlled vocabulary to identify other terms that may be useful to search, for example, *natural disasters* or *oil spills*. The extent of what is called *collocation* (the bringing together of like materials) in the database will depend on the relative intervention of humans or computers in the development of the database.

Klaus establishes that research students may see the controlled vocabulary as:

- *Indistinguishable.* When working from this perspective, students are unaware of the existence of the controlled language and have a naïve view of the language necessary for interaction with the research literature. When students have no understanding of how the database is controlled, they are likely to generate topic-related keywords and trust that when these are entered into the database, they will retrieve a list for browsing. Students' focus is on processing or scanning very large sets of retrieved records for relevant material.

- *Inseparable.* When working from this perspective, students are aware of the existence of the thesaurus and consider it to be inseparable. The controlled language may be used either to establish the relevance of retrieved material (relevant descriptors or keywords appear on the record) or as a catalyst for discovering further material (unanticipated descriptors or keywords are discovered on a record and used for further searching). Students focus on the language contained in the database

- *Separable.* When working from this perspective, students are aware of the controlled vocabulary as being an entity separate from the database; it is seen as an organizing device and a means of communication. When using this lens, students are likely to thoroughly explore the online version of the controlled vocabulary to optimize their searching and the database's response. Some students will discern the limitations of the database and recognize the need to think further about the meaning of the concept for which they are searching. They see the need to look beyond the system to the understandings established in the community

Help Your Students by Thinking and Talking Together About These Questions
- What language are you using as you write about your research?
- What language is being used by colleagues writing in the same area?
- What language are you and your students using to search for relevant resources in the library or on the net?

of experts. Students' focus is on both the language of the database and the broader language of their research community.

Discuss with a librarian where you might need to be aware of which databases you and your students use have controlled language associated with them, and which do not.

Informed Learning Is Reflective About Information Practices

As I have showed in chapter 4, it is possible to devise models grounded in students' experiences to help facilitate reflection and to bring about those experiences that we would wish learners to enter into. Research students' ways of seeing the literature review can also be developed into a reflective model where, together with personal information styles or heuristics, they form the centerpiece of the reflective process (see figure 8.1).

Students may be prompted with reflective questions based on the full range of experiences, thus encouraging them to embrace all facets of the phenomenon. Questions that I have developed for students in many disciplines over the years include the following.

Figure 8.1 Reflective model for reviewing the literature (adapted from Bruce, 1996)

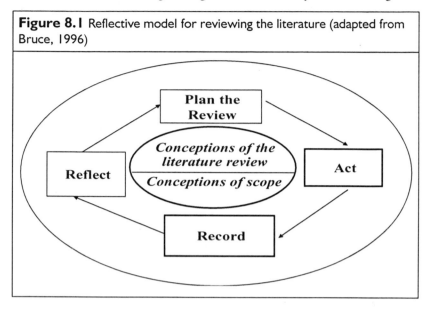

Questions to Help Planning the Literature Review
- What is a literature review, and why am I doing one? (personal reflection on the phenomenon)
- What resources do I have already? (list)
- What should I be looking for now, where do I need to search, and what do I need to do to identify materials? (search)
- What are the key areas relevant to my investigation, and what sort of materials do I need to include or exclude? (survey)
- What do I need to learn about? What ideas am I hoping to test? (vehicle for learning)
- What aspects of my research need direction or support? (facilitator)
- What are my views about the literature, and how should I report them? (report)

Questions to Help Developing the Literature Review
- How can the design of my literature review be improved? Do I need to work on the structure and argument? (reflection on the whole phenomenon)
- What is the present state of my list of references or bibliography? Which areas may need to be brought up-to-

date? Are there any weaknesses that need to be overcome? (list)

- What literature searching have I done in the past two weeks? Are there any new areas that I have become interested in that I may need to search around? (search)
- What have I read recently? Have I found time to read recently? (survey)
- What have I discovered from my reading in the past two weeks? How has my understanding of the area in which I am working developed or changed? (vehicle for learning)
- How could what I have read influence my research? Has my reading inspired me with any ideas that I need to consider, develop, or incorporate? (facilitator)
- Have I been writing about what I have read? Do I need to reconsider how what I have been reading fits into my research? (report)

I have invited students to use these questions in workshops and for personal reflection with their supervisors. Each of the questions is designed to focus attention on a particular experience of the literature review and more broadly to ensure that research students take a 360-degree view of the part of their process that has the potential to deeply influence their research program.

Is There a Possible Relationship Between Information Use and the Learning-to-Research Experience?

Just as we can suggest a relationship between ways of using information and learning, we can also consider the possibility of a relationship between ways of using information and learning to research. While we have no research outcomes upon which to draw, my experience as a supervisor suggests the following.

Ways of Seeing Particular Information Practices May Be Related to Approach to Research
It is possible that particular conceptions of research, as identified by Brew (2001), may be associated with the different ways of experiencing an information practice. For example, conceptions of research may be linked with conceptions of the literature review in these ways:

- The domino conception of research may be linked to the list and search conceptions of literature reviews.
- The layer conception of research may be linked to the survey conception of literature reviews.
- The journey conception of research may be linked to vehicle for learning and research facilitator conceptions of literature reviews.
- The trading conception of research may be linked to the report conception of literature reviews.

Research Students' Ways of Seeing Research and Their Territory or Object May Be Related to Their Engagement With the Information Environment

In the previous chapter, I proposed that researchers' ways of seeing their research territories may influence the way in which information informs their work. The same is also possible for research students. Their view of their research territory may influence

- what information they might see, or be willing to see;
- how they interact with that information;
- how they judge the relevance of the information;
- how they judge or otherwise use the information;
- the character of the new information or knowledge that they generate.

My own research students mainly work in, or across, the field of information technology. Research that I conducted with colleagues shows us that research students in information technology may see their research as being about software development, information practice, human-technology interaction, the application of information technology to other disciplines, or the social impact of technology. Some of them consider that information technology research is what expert others declare to be information technology research. Other students, like their more experienced counterparts, consider themselves to be evolving the field (Bruce, Stoodley & Pham, 2007, manuscript, see chapter 7).

As a supervisor, I recognize that each of these subareas that students see as comprising the territory of IT research has a different research base, a different information environment. Our students' interpretation of what forms their research territory may lead to their admitting different forms of information, research output, and methodologies as relevant to their research endeavor. For example, software engineers creating learning tools may not immediately perceive the relevance of research into students' experience of learning or the possible use of the outcomes of such research in the design of such tools. Similarly, students researching IT learning may not see the relevance of research into intelligent tutoring. Nevertheless, a broader interpretation of the research territory leads to more effective cross-fertilization.

My role, as a supervisor taking forward the informed learning agenda, is

- to understand the interrelationship between students' perception of their field and their experiences with information, as well as the potential impact on the outcomes of their research; and

- to challenge them to adopt more fruitful views of their territory, and at the same time engage with a wider informational context.

Key Questions Arising From This Chapter—What Can We as Educators Do to Take This Agenda Further?

Thinking about students' experience of informed learning in the higher-degree research context can lead to strategies for supporting students and deepening our understanding of their processes.

Informed Learning and Your Philosophy of Supervision
- What information practices are important to you as a researcher and supervisor?
- As a researcher, what do you experience as information?
- As a supervisor, what would you like your students to experience as information?

Informed Learning and Your Students
- Which of the Seven Faces of Informed Learning are your students comfortable with?
- How can you help them to adopt the full range of experiences?
- What do your students experience as information?
- Which ways of seeing the literature review are adopted by your students? Which would you choose to encourage at different stages of the research journey?

- Are there other ways of seeing the literature review important to your discipline?

Informed Learning and Your Supervisory Practice or Pedagogy of Supervision

- How can you use the Seven Faces to influence your supervisory practice?
- How can you encourage the adoption of faces that you prefer your students to be working through at particular times?
- How can you draw students to different ways of thinking about their research object and territory?
- What strategies can you use to draw attention to the possibility of students' views of research or their territory influencing their chosen information environment?

References

Brew, A. (2001). Conceptions of research: A phenomenographic study. *Studies in Higher Education, 26*(3), 271–285.

Bruce, C. S. (1994). Research students' early experiences of the dissertation literature review. *Studies in Higher Education, 19*(2), 217–30.

Bruce, C. S. (1996). From neophyte to expert: Counting on reflection to facilitate complex conceptions of the literature review. In O. Zuber-Skerritt (Ed.), *Frameworks for postgraduate supervision and research* (pp. 239–253), Lismore, New South Wales, Australia: Southern Cross University Press.

Bruce, C. S. (2001). Interpreting the scope of their literature reviews: Significant differences in research students' concerns. *New Library World, 102*(4/5), 158–165.

Bruce, C. S., Stoodley, I., & Pham, B. (2007, manuscript). Constituting information technology research: The experience of IT research students.

Klaus, H. (2000). Understanding scholarly and professional communication. In C. Bruce & P. Candy (Eds.), *Information literacy around the world: Advances in programs and research* (pp. 209–222). Riverina, Australia: Centre for Information Studies, Charles Sturt University.

Meyer, J., Shanahan, M., & Laugksch, R. (2005). Students' conceptions of research. I: A qualitative and quantitative analysis. *Scandinavian Journal of Educational Research, 49*, 225–244.

Wood, K. (2006). Changing as a person: The experience of learning to research in the social sciences. *Higher Education Research and Development, 25*(1), 53–66.

Chapter 9

Championing Informed Learning Across the Organization

Opening Narrative

Jane and Steve are being asked to influence the wider community. It is a few years since they started life as academics. They have been promoted to senior positions and are now expected to take a stronger lead in influencing policy in their departments and among their colleagues. They are each responsible for programs of study and are often invited to talk about their curriculum work with information practices and to encourage their colleagues in other faculties to also explore learning strategies that draw on information practices in their disciplines. Jane and Steve's institution and many others now have policies around informed learning, or information literacy education, requiring learners to become creative, reflective, and ethical information users as part of their university experience.

Steve and Jane need to consider the range of stakeholders involved in the process and the kinds of organizational culture required for such learning design to be possible. Not everyone in the academic community is aware of the importance of building information practices into curriculum or of the need to enhance students' awareness of the information environment and their interaction with it. Steve and Jane host a symposium opened by the Pro Vice Chancellor Teaching and Learning and the University Librarian to symbolize the unified character of informed learning. They invite colleagues and students to discuss their experience and invite researchers and teaching fellows to conduct workshops that would be of interest to teachers from different discipline backgrounds.

What conditions need to be put into place for informed learning to thrive? How can different members of the university and other learning communities work together to promote informed learning? In this chapter, I explore how we might influence our organizations, raising awareness of informed learning. I propose the RACER approach to bringing about change. The RACER approach identifies five points of focus: Recognize different roles and perspectives, Accept diversity, Change with support, Engage in the scholarship of teaching, and Research the future. I then look at how the Six Frames and Seven Faces models might be used to promote teaching excellence, and I highlight research insights into disciplinary perspectives on information literacy pedagogy.

Informed Learning Across the University: Constituting the Collective Awareness

Bringing about change is a major undertaking in whatever context it needs to occur. Advocates of new approaches to curriculum or learning need to be aware of what it takes to bring about change. What conditions should be put in place for new directions, such as informed learning, to thrive?

As we assume the role of advocates and champions for teaching excellence, promoting informed learning, we can adopt a relational approach to such advocacy. This would involve seeing our role as influencing the collective awareness of the organization through targeting staff learning at both the individual and the collective levels.

Bowden and Marton (1998) describe the character of collective awareness in relation to learning and research. They describe the former as "the degree of awareness among teachers and students of the other's ways of seeing," and the latter as "the degree of awareness amongst researchers and graduate students of the others' ways of seeing" (p. 196). The idea of collective awareness is also interpreted at the organizational level. Here it is described in terms of the extent to which members of an organization are "conscious (aware) of the ways in which phenomena of common concern appear to other members" (p. 201). The collective awareness comprises both what is common and what is complementary. For the organization to benefit, these different ways of thinking must be brought into focus.

In relation to furthering the use of informed learning, influencing an organization's or department's collective consciousness means

- bringing informed learning into focus
- raising awareness of common and complementary ways of seeing informed learning across the organization

As I have already suggested, this may be achieved by targeting staff learning at both the individual and collective levels. Here, learning at the collective level occurs as staff share their differing understandings of their professional practice and as the university community moves towards shared understandings of learning and important associated phenomena such as informed learning (Bruce, Chesterton, & Grimison, 2002).

The RACER Approach to Bringing About Curriculum Change

Informed learning, like many other innovative approaches, is likely to thrive only in a culture that values teaching and learning. The RACER approach proposes a broad framework that requires strong commitment to quality teaching and learning at the organizational level. It also suggests key strategies for bringing informed learning into focus and continuing to focus on informed learning in different aspects of the teaching and learning culture. The five components of the RACER approach are:

1. Recognize different roles and perspectives
2. Accept diversity
3. Change with support
4. Engage in the scholarship of teaching—including evaluation
5. Research for the future

While the RACER approach is described here with particular attention to a university or college environment, it may be easily adapted to other organizations or workplaces that promote informed learning.

RACER is intended to support an institutional commitment to informed learning or information literacy that comprises four interrelated and interdependent parts:

- Resources that facilitate the learning of specific skills, for example, packages to enhance Web-based information skills
- Curricula that provide the opportunity to learn specific skills from self-paced packages, lecturers, librarians, or peers
- Curricula that include learning activities that require the use of academic, discipline-specific, or professional information practices
- Curricula that require reflection on the experience of informed learning

Recognize Different Roles and Perspectives

Informed learning is a shared responsibility. In developing a culture supportive of informed learning, we need to recognize the part played by many individuals and organizational units, not only within the university, but also in industry and the community. Many roles and partnerships between people make it possible to bring information practices into the curriculum. It is therefore it necessary for someone in the advocacy role to work both vertically and horizontally across the organizational structure.

Successful informed learning initiatives bring about curriculum change. In figure 9.1 below, curriculum is depicted at the core of the framework required for successful initiatives. Supporting curriculum are partnerships between teachers and information and IT professionals, including librarians. Supporting those partnerships are institutional policies and the information and IT infrastructures necessary to informed learning.

Usually information and IT infrastructures are largely in place for the purposes of informed learning. Where they are not, substantial planning and budgets may be required to secure them over an extended period.

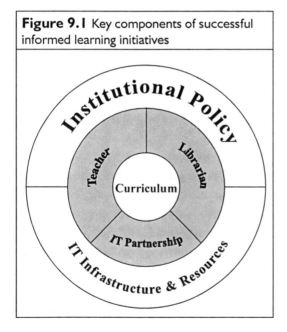

Figure 9.1 Key components of successful informed learning initiatives

Informed learning initiatives can also be supported by broad policies around graduate capabilities and lifelong learning. This broader focus provides an important context for informed learning. Promotion of informed learning can also be integrated with the broader philosophies and values of the university. We can pay attention not only to benefits to industry, the economy, and individuals seeking professional currency and renewal, but also to the empowering features of informed learning in community and personal contexts, to social justice issues, and to the ethical dimensions of informed learning.

> **Tips for Championing Teaching Excellence Through Informed Learning**
> Use course approval and review processes to monitor the inclusion of informed learning in curricula. Ensure that policy and resources support the desired directions.

Accept Diversity—Including in the Student Body
Diversity in views and approaches is something to be celebrated, and in an environment that values creativity and reflection, it should never be discouraged. In encouraging the adoption of informed learning, we are likely to encounter diversity in many forms, all of which should be acknowledged and allowed to contribute to the wider organizational direction. We will encounter diversity in:

- *Colleagues' diverse views of informed learning and how to teach for informed learning.* As I have shown in earlier chapters, many different experiences contribute to the broad academic, professional, and civic experience of informed learning. Everyone involved brings their own experiences to the informed learning agenda and has their own views of how best to teach towards that agenda. As I have also shown in earlier chapters, it is important to allow different views to coexist and to bring them together in curriculum in ways that will facilitate planned learning outcomes. The most important decisions in curriculum change tend to be around relative emphasis on particular views, rather than choosing one view over another.

- *The diverse roles that may be adopted by ourselves and others as change agents.* Bringing about change also requires many roles. Staff may find themselves required to carry out the functions of quality assurers, innovators, or facilitators. They may also find themselves cast in these roles by colleagues. Most of us find that we prefer to work in particular ways as change agents, and we may need to become conscious of our style and be willing to modify it to meet the needs of those around us. Alternatively, we may need to identify partners to assume the different functions.

- *The diverse motivations of participants.* Colleagues will choose to participate in the informed learning agenda for many reasons. Why might they become involved? Perhaps because they want to, because they enjoy experimentation, because they have to, because they can see benefits to their students, or because they see benefits to their own career path. An emphasis on engaging with the scholarship of teaching (see below) can often accommodate a wide range of needs and motivations.

• *Students' needs and motivations.* Students engaged in informed learning will also have multiple needs and motivations, partly as a result of ever-increasing diversity in the student body. Student diversity may stem from gender, cultural backgrounds, family circumstances, work commitments, or technological affinity, among other factors. Encouraging staff and students to place some emphasis on the Personal Relevance frame for informed learning and to use portfolios for some aspects of assessment can help draw students' attention to the ways in which their needs are being addressed.

Tips for Championing Teaching Excellence Through Informed Learning

Capture diverse approaches to informed learning by electronically showcasing a portfolio of strategies, including student work.

Change with Support

In order to achieve support for informed learning, it can be useful to consider the following values as programs are developed and implemented. These "enablers of successful programmes" (Bruce, Chesterton, & Grimison, 2002) were identified as part of a university-wide implementation of a curriculum-change initiative supporting the integration and embedding of information use:

• *Inclusiveness* ensures that staff from different disciplines and departments across the organization are involved.

• *Comprehensiveness* ensures that all sites or campuses have the opportunity to participate.

• *Management* ensures that horizontal and vertical communication strategies are implemented across the institution and departments.

• *Choice* offers different approaches to learning and involvement.

• *Cooperation* brings together members of different parts of the organization in a collaborative effort to effecting change.

• *Participation* emphasizes action and engagement: emphasizes teachers making changes to their curriculum and teaching practice.

- *Modeling* models informed learning, by adopting inquiry, re-source-based, or other processes as key strategies.

The adoption of informed learning is most likely to take root in contexts where there is simultaneous emphasis on educational best practice. This will often involve encouraging a shift from a content approach towards a stronger process approach in teaching and encouraging a shift from a teacher-centered to a learner-centered view of learning. Increased emphasis on understanding the perceptual worlds of students and their pedagogical implications is also important. It is important that, in informed learning, content and process are simultaneous and not competing foci; it remains true, however, that to allow this simultaneous emphasis, it is likely to be necessary to put aside some content.

Teachers who value learner-centered approaches find it much easier to embrace informed learning. In helping colleagues to move forward with informed learning, there are usually several hurdles to overcome, where many teachers are likely to need support:

- Understanding that information literacy is not a prerequisite to learning. We are not talking about a program of remediation, but rather about actualizing a way of learning.
- Modifying, changing, or constructing new designs for learning experiences.
- Changing how much we expect students to learn. In a process approach, content is no longer paramount; rather, ability to learn is.
- Technology: learning to use technology and learning to use technology to support learning.

Tips for Championing Teaching Excellence Through Informed Learning

Reward interest in informed learning by requesting attention to this aspect of learning in teaching excellence award criteria.

Engage in the Scholarship of Teaching—Including Evaluation
Encouraging engagement in the scholarship of teaching is a critical component of taking forward the informed learning agenda at an organizational level. In its most complex form, the scholarship of teaching is research, where teachers investigate aspects of the learning environment,

seek to bring about change in the pursuit of learning, and subject their efforts to peer scrutiny and review through publication.

The scholarship of teaching, with its intention of making a contribution to the pedagogy of the discipline, is a vital tool for supporting collaboration and innovation. It can be used as a framework to encourage individual and team involvement in the implementation of informed learning and evaluation of processes designed for particular groups of students and their outcomes. As teachers become familiar with the process of reading, designing, investigating, and publishing, they can be encouraged to focus their attention on exploring many dimensions of informed learning, including teachers' perspectives, learners' perspectives, the impact on learning, and strategies for overcoming barriers to new ways of doing things.

Tips for Championing Teaching Excellence Through Informed Learning
Promote informed learning in the scholarship of teaching through teaching and learning grant schemes that encourage application in specific discipline areas.

Research for the Future
The final contributor to developing a culture supportive of informed learning is research. There is much that needs to be subjected to research, both within universities and within the professions and wider community. We need to understand the experience of informed learning further, among different student cohorts and in different professions and disciplines. The experience of informed learning in the community and workplace is also significantly understudied.

There is scope for different types of research undertaken for different purposes by different groups. Informed learning presents a significant opportunity for working within the teaching-research nexus. Classroom teachers may wish to investigate and understand the informed learning experience of their own students and the impact of learning innovations, thus contributing to the research agenda. Outside the classroom, we may wish to undertake larger scale research into the learning experience or into informed learning in the community, workplace, disciplines, and professions, thus contributing to teaching and learning development. Chapter 10 expands the potential for research under the informed learning banner.

> ## Tips for Championing Teaching Excellence Through Informed Learning
> Support the development of teaching and learning research communities, including a focus on informed learning

Informed Learning Is a Shared Responsibility
In summary, informed learning is a shared responsibility, requiring the collaboration and expertise of many members of the teaching and learning community. Discipline teachers, librarians, instructional designers, IT specialists, and others all need to work together to ensure the effective development of informed learning. Librarians are usually willing to play an advisory role or to work in close collaboration with faculty.

Using the Six Frames for Championing Teaching Excellence
The Six Frames for Informed Learning may be used as a tool for the development of strategies to support the change process, including raising awareness about informed learning, and the implementation of programs. In this section, I propose using the frames to enhance partnerships, understand challenges, facilitate curriculum change, and evaluate. Each of these directions is accompanied by suggested workshop activities, which may be used alongside the Six Frames.

For Enhancing Cross-University Partnerships
Groups of staff who assume leadership roles in advocacy for informed learning are often caught in dilemmas of communication and institutional politics. Understanding how different parts of the organization can adopt different perspectives, often resulting in the presence of unusual dynamics, can help leaders better manage the directions they wish to pursue. An example of how the Six Frames may be used with such a group appears below. Teachers, administrators, and librarians participating in such activities have commented on the importance of "becoming aware that my way might not be the only way."

Suggestion for Workshop Design

Participants are asked to bring to the workshop a one-page case description of a problem or issue associated with information literacy or informed learning.

Briefly describe to your partners the case you have brought:

- Identify the key elements of the case, for example, (a) individuals, (b) groups, (c) organizational units, (d) elements of curriculum, (e) policy or guidelines, and (f) other.
- What is the primary frame that is being used by (or that is dominating) each element in your case?

How has using the Six Frames to analyze the problem helped you? What insights have you gained? Have you come to see anything differently? Will you do anything differently as a result?

For Understanding Challenges

Designing programs, teaching, and working with colleagues and students on a day-to-day basis can be frustrating when different people do not appear to share the same ways of thinking about critical issues. Understanding the different points of view that stakeholders in the institution bring to the change agenda can be very useful for helping leaders of change to manage their own contribution and role. An example of how the Six Frames may be used with such a group appears below. Staff that have participated in such activities have commented on the importance of recognizing different perspectives: "Looking at the Frames helps me understand why people have different resistance. Being aware of that will help me."

Suggestion for Workshop Design

Review the Six Frames for Informed Learning and ask these questions:

- What are your preferred primary and secondary frames?
- What are the preferred primary and secondary frames of
  — the students you teach—as a general rule?
  — the academics in this institution—as you see it?
  — the librarians in this institution—as you see it?
  — the institution—as evidenced by policy, curriculum, documents, and so on?

For Facilitating or Enhancing Curriculum Design

In advancing the informed learning agenda, it is always necessary to help teachers design aspects of their curriculum to take the agenda forward. Teachers can be encouraged to intentionally use the different frames in order to achieve different learning outcomes.

Making explicit the frames through which participants might view informed learning could be achieved by sharing the frames (see chapter 2) and inviting participants to identify those frames with which they identify. Examples of learning strategies they already used may illustrate their preferred frames. How might their learning strategies change if they adopted a different frame? Discussion or analysis could focus on the nature of the information practice and content being learned in each strategy. What barriers or supports do participants see as progressing or hindering the agenda in their local context?

Susie Andretta (2008, in press, p. 5) describes how her "educators in training" intentionally used different frames to achieve different learning outcomes. One team used the Relational frame to strengthen the information practices of clinical research physicians. Another team adopted the Competency and Learning to Learn frames to design training in the use of ICTs for the improvement of clinical care.

Suggestion for Workshop Design

Divide participants into small groups and ask group members to talk with each other about an informed learning or information literacy program with which they are familiar (dividing the time equally among members):

- Briefly describe the program.
- For each part of the program that you want to discuss, what is the primary frame that is being used or that is dominating?
- What might the program look like if a different frame was used?

Then ask them to discuss these questions:

- How has using the Six Frames to analyze the program helped you?

An example of how the Six Frames may be used to encourage teachers or program designers to consider a range of approaches to informed learning appears below. Staff participating in such activities have commented on the importance of recognizing different perspectives: "Looking at the frames is like being at the theatre and using frames to change the mood. It can be useful to work through all the frames—I'd like to use them as filters, but not necessarily to keep them all on."

For Evaluation
Participants involved in longer programs could be asked to use the Six Frames to reflect on their position or their current thinking at various points in the program. Alternatively, they could be surveyed to identify which frames they are being most influenced by at strategic points in the training program.

Suggestion for Evaluation Design

Andretta (2008, in press) provides an example of a professional development program for educators where the Six Frames for Informed Learning are used to underpin the program evaluation process. Participants were introduced to the frames in the first of several sessions and invited to identify the two frames they believed themselves to be most influenced by. At this early point in her course, frames 2 and 4 were identified as the most dominant. At the end of the course, most participants were choosing to be influenced by frames 4 and 6.

Using the Seven Faces to Advance the Informed Learning Agenda

Like the Six Frames, the Seven Faces of Informed Learning (chapter 3) can also be used to champion teaching excellence and advance the informed learning agenda. Modules, workshops, and other activities can be developed around the Seven Faces to support awareness raising, reflection, and curriculum design. Important directions for such modules might include

- making explicit participants' own experiences of informed learning;
- strengthening understanding of the Relational frame;
- adapting existing models to participants' discipline contexts;

- considering the impact of existing practice and future possibilities.

Making Explicit Participants' Own Experiences of Informed Learning
This could be achieved by sharing a summary of the Seven Faces, for example, from chapter 3, and inviting participants to share their own narratives to illustrate their experience. Discussion about the similarities and differences between experiences among the group may reveal disciplinary or other contextual influences on informed learning. It may be possible from such discussions among small groups to collect narratives and critiques as an ongoing resource for interested teachers.

Strengthening Understanding of the Relational Frame
This could be achieved by inviting participants to consider the Six Frames and, if they have not already done so, to discuss with colleagues the frames that they are currently using in their teaching. They could then work together to redesign aspects of their curriculum to reflect the Relational frame, using curriculum examples from chapters 2 and 3 to support their activity if they wish.

Adapting Existing Models to Participants' Discipline Contexts
This involves finding time and space for colleagues in a discipline to work together to elaborate aspects of informed learning as it may appear in their field. Can the Seven Faces of Informed Learning be adapted for the discipline? Do different forms of experience need to be described? What are the information practices that need to be mastered in the discipline? What contents can be pursued through these practices? Possible outcomes of such discussion might be the construction of informed learning applicable to specific discipline and course contexts and a growing pool of possible teaching strategies.

Considering the Impact of Existing Practice and Future Possibilities
This involves reviewing existing curriculum and learning strategies to identify where students are already engaging in informed learning and how such learning might be strengthened. Possible outcomes might be new or modified learning objectives, learning strategies, or assessment strategies that encourage students to be aware of and reflect on their

information practices. Curriculum could be benchmarked against each of the Seven Faces for this exercise. It is important to note here that only whole programs are likely to represent all of the Seven Faces.

Championing Teaching Excellence Through Informed Learning: An Example From the University of the West of England

Jackie Chelin and Stewart Green have worked to enhance teaching and learning through information literacy in their university. Below, they document their experience of championing the relational approach and of working with colleagues who are bringing different curriculum frames to the table:

"... a small group of academic and library staff has been dedicated both to raising the awareness of information literacy among academic and library staff, and to encouraging the university to consider the development of information literacy as it develops new strategies in relation to teaching, learning, assessment, research and knowledge exchange.

"To date the main tactics for achieving these two goals have been research by the group into the notion of information literacy, the staging of two university workshops in order to disseminate the results of this research, and the inclusion of information literacy as a key learning outcome in the specification of a new programme (see below) that will be taken by all students in each of their three years of study.

"Research by the group quickly identified two prominent approaches to information literacy: the SCONUL model (http://www.sconul.ac.uk/) based upon a series of increasingly complex information skills, and the relational approach—as described in *The Seven Faces of Information Literacy* (1997)—based upon seven different ways of conceiving information literacy. While some members of staff felt very comfortable with the skills based approach, others were swayed by the appeal of the relational approach with its underpinning theory of phenomenography, its framework of conceptions, its guide for curriculum design, and its outline of a programme of research. But, unfortunately, the latter group had difficulty locating studies in the literature that illustrated effective practical use of the relational approach in teaching, which impeded its appeal to the wider community.

"This problem led us to introduce as a key goal for our second workshop the improvement of our understanding of the relational approach. This goal was addressed first by the inclusion in the workshop of the visiting keynote speaker's work on the association of particular conceptions of information literacy with particular academic disciplines (Webber, Boon, & Johnston, 2005, 2006). It was further addressed by a presentation of the use of reflective practice throughout a level-three UWE module. In this module conceptions of information literacy related in particular to critical thinking, e.g., evaluating, extending and creating knowledge, are further developed in students.

"A new programme has been designed at UWE that will be taken by all students in all three years of their study. This course has thirteen learning outcomes related to topics such as group learning, programme coherence, feedback, and employability. The information literacy group has ensured that one of the key learning outcomes covers information literacy: viz 'to reflect on and summarise their [students'] ability to find, evaluate, abstract and analyse information in relation to their programme.' The incorporation of this learning outcome in this course will ensure that all UWE students are exposed to some level of provision of information literacy; and this provision will augment provision from their other programme modules.

"Of course, this does not necessarily mean that information literacy will be delivered by the relational approach. However, as we learn more about the relational approach and its relationship to the information skills approach, the potential for the former to have an increasing influence on the provision of information literacy at UWE is likely to grow.

"As one of the most controversial discussion points from the second IL seminar was the difficulty of meaningfully defining IL, it was suggested that academic and library staff within particular faculties might find it useful to meet, to debate, to identify and hopefully to agree their conceptions of IL within their particular subject areas as a basis for taking it forward in a more planned and co-ordinated way with students." (Jackie Chelin & Stewart Green, e-mail communication, July 2007)

Information-Literacy Pedagogy: Discipline-Based Experiences

Many of the suggestions in the earlier parts of this chapter encourage the contextualization of the informed learning agenda. Just as using information to learn is experienced differently, it is also learned differently and taught differently.

Working within specific disciplines, Sheila Webber, Stuart Boon, and Bill Johnston have begun to show, through empirical research, how university teachers' ways of seeing information literacy and their ways of seeing teaching for information literacy are connected. In chapter 2, I looked at how different approaches to teaching and learning, and to information literacy, might influence teaching practice around informed learning on the basis of broad curriculum frameworks.

In this section, I summarize Webber, Boon, and Johnston's emerging insights into information-literacy pedagogy in discipline contexts. Each of their publications summarized is referenced below. These insights confirm the importance of ensuring that, as we advocate for informed learning and champion change, people have the opportunity to reflect on their own position and relate discussion of informed learning to their own disciplines. While we do not yet have detailed data around many disciplines, the verification of differences in some contexts reinforces that disciplinary differences are to be expected, can be made explicit, and will drive individual and curricular agendas.

Pedagogical Perspectives from Chemistry
Teachers of chemistry (Webber & Johnston, 2007) may reveal the following range of approaches to teaching information literacy, each of which is associated with particular learning outcomes being sought. Teaching information literacy may be seen as:

- *Implicit in teaching students to understand chemistry.* In this view, teaching information literacy is an integral, and indistinguishable, part of learning chemistry. Teachers make the assumption that students have the information skills they need, but will provide coaching when deficiencies are detected. The learning outcome sought is mastering information skills required for chemistry.
- *Designing a path for students through a chemistry course.* In this view, teaching information literacy is seen as separate from teaching chemistry. Teachers provide relevant experiences, explicitly required by

curriculum, to ensure students master information skills. The learning outcome sought is becoming workplace-ready, independent information seekers and problem solvers.

• *Challenging students to respond independently, critically, and creatively.* In this view, teaching information literacy is seen as separate from teaching chemistry and is also seen as a key contributor to communicating and creating knowledge. The learning outcomes sought involve developing creative, exploratory characteristics, changing as a person, and enjoying the process.

Pedagogical Perspectives from Marketing

Teachers of marketing (Webber, Boon & Johnston, 2006) may reveal the following range of approaches to teaching information literacy.

• *Someone else's job.* In this view, teachers of marketing see information literacy as a set of skills that it is not their responsibility to teach. When seeing this way, teachers focus on their discipline content.

• *Upgrading students' information toolbox.* In this view, teachers of marketing see information literacy as skills that they need to provide, and therefore their responsibility as teachers is to introduce students to relevant processes required for completing set learning tasks. When seeing this way, teachers focus on the relationship between skills and the course of study

• *Facilitating access to a variety of resources.* In this view, teachers of marketing see information literacy as having easy access to information and therefore see teaching for information literacy as making relevant resources available. When seeing this way, teachers focus on their role in providing information access.

• *Showing students how and when to use information skills.* In this view, teachers see teaching for information literacy as being about recognizing and meeting students' needs. When seeing this way, teachers focus on providing skills when students need them.

• *Helping students to understand how information literacy is critical to them.* Teachers may see teaching for information literacy as using a range of strategies to encourage students to see the value of information literacy. When seeing this way, teachers focus on the importance of information literacy in the discipline or professional practice.

Pedagogical Perspectives from English
Teachers of English (Webber, Boon, & Johnston, 2006) may reveal the following range of approaches to teaching information literacy:

- *Someone else's job.* They may see information literacy as a set of skills that it is not their responsibility to teach. When seeing this way, teachers focus on their discipline content.

- *An add-on or side effect to teaching their subject.* They may see information literacy as skills that students gain independently through the completion of assignments. Teaching information literacy in this view appears to center around setting relevant tasks. When seeing this way, teachers focus on course requirements

- *Introducing students to sources of information.* Where information literacy is seen as research skills, then teaching for information literacy becomes teaching students about, or giving them exposure to, appropriate information sources. When seeing this way, teachers focus on introducing information sources.

- *Engaging with students to show them the value of information and information literacy.* Teaching for information literacy may also be seen as bringing students into an understanding and awareness of the importance of information and information literacy for their own personal growth and academic development. When seeing this way, teachers focus on engaging with students.

Key Questions Arising From This Chapter—What Can We as Educators Do to Take This Agenda Further?

Informed Learning and Your Development Practice

- What aspects of informed learning are already visible in your development practice?
- How can you work with other staff to take forward the informed learning agenda?
- How can you influence policy, curriculum design, or evaluation frameworks to progress interest in informed learning?
- How can you integrate an interest in informed learning into existing development practices?
- What new practices may be valuable to pursue?

Informed Learning and Your Organization
- How could the collective consciousness of informed learning be developed?
- What aspects of informed learning are already a part of the organization's development program?
- Which aspects of the RACER model are already in place (perhaps partly) in your organization?
- Which aspects need to be taken forward, and how could this be done?
- What strategies could be put in place to simultaneously encourage teaching and learning best practice and the progression of informed learning?

References

Andretta, S. (2008, in press). Facilitating Information Literacy Education (FILE). In A. Brine (Ed.), *Handbook of library training practice and development, (Vol. 3)*. Aldershot, England: Gower Publishing Ltd.

Bowden, J., & Marton, F. (1998). *The university of learning: Beyond quality and competence in higher education*. London: Kogan Page.

Bruce, C., Chesterton, P., & Grimison, C. (2002). Constituting collective consciousness: Information literacy in university curricula. *The International Journal of Academic Development, 7*(1), 31–40.

Webber, S., Boon, S., & Johnston, B. (2005). A comparison of UK academics' conceptions of information literacy in two disciplines: English and marketing. *Library and Information Research, 29*(93), 4–15.

Webber, S., Boon, S., & Johnston, B. (2006). British academics from different disciplines: Comparing their conceptions of pedagogy for information literacy. English version of Comparison des conceptions pédagogiques de la maîtrise de l'information chez des universitaires britanniques de différentes disciplines. In *Actes des Semes Rencontres Formist: Lyon: 2005*. Lyon. ESSIB. Available at http://www.enssib.fr/bibliotheque-numerique/document-1172

Webber, S., & Johnston, B. (2007). Chemistry academics' conceptions of teaching chemistry: Conceptions and implications. Paper presented at I3, Information: Interactions and Impact, conference held at the Department of Information Management, Aberdeen Business School, The Robert Gordon University, Aberdeen, UK, June 25–28, 2007.

Chapter 10

Informed Learning: A Research Agenda

Opening Narrative

Steve and Jane decide that they should start researching in the area of their teaching interest. If their students' interaction with their information worlds appears to have a significant impact on their learning, and if research to date is supporting this possibility, then for them it may be a fruitful area to pursue.

When they get started, they find that their work transcends disciplinary boundaries,, drawing on and belonging to more than one field: learning in higher education, learning in their discipline, information use, and ICT literacies, among others. This is an enjoyable experience, but also challenging because they need to belong to multiple research communities, not all of which are immediately sympathetic to their research. They also find that within their immediate academic environment, it is unclear whether their work is research into the teaching of the discipline or closely tied to the discipline itself.

Steve and Jane decide to work collaboratively here because this approach will help to reveal the cross-disciplinary nature of their work. They apply for teaching fellowships and research grants. They consider teaming up with colleagues working in the education and ICT disciplines. Larger teams are more complex, but the members will bring their complementary strengths to the work. Steve and Jane also find that there are many instructional designers and information professionals, librarians, and information and knowledge managers who have serious scholarly interests in this field. Some are colleagues who already have grants or teaching fellowships through which they are pursuing their interests.

Informed learning has taken form through problemetizing using information for learning and applying the idea that learning is about experiencing variation to that problem. Implementation and ongoing development of informed learning rest on furthering our understanding of using information to learn in different contexts. In this chapter, I propose a research agenda that may be contributed to by members of all disciplines, by researchers into information literacy, information, and learning.

Researching Variation in the Experience of Informed Learning

As I have presented it in this book, informed learning problemetizes using information for learning and applies the idea that learning is about experiencing variation to that problem in a sustained way. It is an attempt to tackle this question: *What does it mean to consider information literacy and learning simultaneously from the perspective of those experiencing the information literacy and learning?* The idea that learning is about experiencing variation, or coming to see the phenomena being learned about differently by coming to focus on its critical aspects, is the foundational idea of variation theory. The variation theory of learning and its associated research approach, phenomenography, are described in detail by Ference Marton and Shirley Booth in their seminal book, *Learning and Awareness* (1997).

Interest in uncovering critical differences in ways of experiencing various phenomena, such as information literacy, Internet searching, and the relationship between information literacy and learning, has guided many of the research projects reported in earlier chapters; these projects rely heavily on the constructs outlined in *Learning and Awareness*. The later chapters around higher-degree research and development strategies for staff are inspired by John Bowden and Ference Marton's application of the ideas established in *Learning and Awareness* to the research context in the subsequent publication, the *University of Learning* (Bowden & Marton, 1998). In their book, Bowden and Marton propose the idea of research as learning at the collective level, where changes in ways of seeing phenomenon constitute a contribution to knowledge, They also propose the idea of the collective consciousness of a community as being about the extent to which variation in ways of seeing are shared across a group. Their thinking has substantially influenced the development of my ideas about informed learning in the research and academic-development contexts.

In this book, I have emphasized the value of researching variation in experience as a tool for uncovering critical differences; which can be then used as an aid in promoting informed learning. Researching variation in the experience of informed learning draws extensively on the phenomenographic approach to research as described and discussed in *Learning and Awareness* (Marton & Booth, 1997). The primary intent of the phenomenographic approach is to uncover the learners' understanding or experience from the point of view of those learners. It is this fresh understanding of learners' experiences that then makes it possible for us to help them learn. Many of the studies used as examples in this book have adopted this research perspective.

Some phenomenographers have now adopted "new phenomenography," which involves studying the way in which learning is enacted by students and teachers in the classroom. How is the space of variation opened up by teachers, and how is it understood by learners? (Marton & Tsui, 2004). Taking research steps in this direction, Louise Limberg and colleagues have been exploring how school teachers and librarians teach information seeking, treating information seeking as an aspect of information literacy (Limberg & Folkesson, 2006).

The phenomenographic approach and variation theory are likely to continue to offer a great deal to the informed learning agenda, as they make possible two important types of research outcomes. First, they provide strategies for understanding student learning in a unique way; second, they provide a framework for bringing about learning once critical differences in students' experience have been understood.

Key Concepts Associated With Informed Learning: Elements of a Research Agenda

Informed learning is also the outworking of an interest in people's experience of information literacy and information-literacy education. It is an extension of the Relational model for information literacy and information-literacy education (Bruce, 1997). The Relational model emphasizes the importance of uncovering variation and establishes the importance of (a) interpreting the phenomena of *information use* and *information* from an experiential or relational perspective, and (b) interpreting information-literacy education as bringing people's information practices (professional, disciplinary, or civic) into the curriculum.

Earlier chapters of this book showed that a range of key concepts contribute to the idea of informed learning. In this book, I have used the term *informed learning* to refer to both an approach to learning and the experience of learning through information use. Here I look at how several contributing concepts may be teased apart. The most vexed term below is *information literacy*, which in the literature is variously interpreted as *information skills*, *using information to learn*, or sometimes even *information-literacy education*. In this book, I have emphasized the orientation towards *using information to learn* by preferring the term *informed learning* and using it instead of *information literacy*. To illustrate the subtle distinction between informed learning and information literacy, the idea of informed learning may be compared with the idea of problem-based learning; to extend that analogy, information literacy is akin to problem-solving ability (see table 1.1).

All these concepts are important elements of the informed learning research agenda:

- **Informed learning:** using information to learn.
- **Informed learners:** people who engage with the different ways of using information to learn (i.e., information literacy).
- **Learning:** coming to see or experience the world in new ways. This may be developing expert views or creating new ways of seeing.
- **Information literacy:** experiencing different ways of using information to learn.
- **Information literacy education:** enabling students to work with the different ways of using information to learn; the educational framework that makes it possible for students to experience information literacy in new ways.
- **Learning information literacy:** coming to experience information literacy in new ways.
- **Information:** anything that we experience as informing. Information will appear differently in different contexts and different disciplines.
- **Information use:** interacting with information; an expression or visible enactment of information literacy.
- **Information practices:** the practical processes and contexts within which information is used, for example, professional development, essay writing, research, composition, Internet searching.
- **Information skills:** the building blocks, the personal capabilities that make information literacy possible, in the

same way that the ability to read and write makes literate practice possible.

- **Information technology:** the systems or infrastructure, including mobile devices, that enable different forms of information use.

Current Directions in Informed Learning Research

Information-literacy research forms the cornerstone of existing research underpinning informed learning. Information-literacy research is interdisciplinary, being influenced primarily by learning theory and the broader domain of educational research, and secondarily by other fields, such as information seeking and use, information behavior, psychology, literacy, health, and management, to name a few. Key investigations into the experience of information literacy have begun to establish several trajectories, some of which have been highlighted in previous chapters, including:

- The experience of information literacy from a cross-disciplinary perspective (chapter 3)
- Discipline-specific experiences of information literacy from students' perspectives (chapter 4)
- Students' experiences of information literacy (chapter 4)
- Students' experience of particular information practices (chapter 4)
- Discipline-specific experiences of information literacy from academic perspectives (chapter 5)
- Professional experiences of information literacy (chapter 6)
- Community information literacy (chapter 6)
- Research students' experiences of information practices (chapter 8)
- Pedagogy for information literacy (chapter 9)

These experience-based investigations have deepened our understanding of the phenomenon of information literacy. Other information-literacy research has involved the application of a range of approaches to specific problems, such as extensive surveys of students' literacies and skills, the use of action research to investigate the impact of information literacy education, and the investigation of learners' knowledge structures (see Bruce, 2000).

Future Directions for Informed Learning Research

In this chapter, I focus on establishing a broad agenda for informed learning research, which may be attended to by a multiplicity of approaches. What we research and how we research it usually go together. Just as we can frame informed learning through exploring different approaches that may be adopted to teaching, learning, information, and information literacy, we can also frame research into informed learning by exploring different approaches that may be adopted to research.

Many approaches will be taken in future to researching informed learning. Researchers who see informed learning and information literacy as quantifiable and measurable are likely to adopt observable and measurable behavior as their research object. Researchers who see informed learning and information literacy as contextualized and deeply embedded in professional, academic, and disciplinary practices are likely to adopt lived experience as their research object. Both approaches, and different positions in between, will contribute to our unfolding understanding of informed learning. So far, it is the experiential, interpretive approaches that give us insights into people's experience, that have laid the foundation for the emergence of the concept of informed learning.

Researching informed learning must take us across a wide range of spaces, understanding the rich and the poor, the digitally enabled and the digitally disabled, the psychologically empowered and the psychologically disempowered. How do people use information to learn in their many and varied circumstances and contexts?

Researching people's experience and taking a second-order perspective (looking at the world from the perspective of the people participating) allow us to avoid imposing norms about information and information use that have evolved in developed, high-technology contexts. As Joan Challinor so eloquently comments, "It is now past time to accept an 'information literacy super-highway' on which men in the developed world, and some in the developing world, are traveling in fast cars while the majority of women in the developing world are walking barefoot on dirt-roads." Citing the 68 Digital Opportunities task force, she reminds us that our purpose is: "… to help the poorest help themselves to create richer and fuller lives that express and affirm their own distinctiveness in an increasingly interconnected global village" (in Thompson, 2003, pp. 24–25).

Further implementation and development of the informed learning project rests on furthering our insights into information literacy or informed learning in academic, community, and workplace contexts.

At its core, informed learning research is focused on *using information to learn*. Research into informed learning should continue to bridge multiple domains—learning, information, technology, information literacy, communication, media studies, and the relevant discipline, professional, or community context of interest. Research into informed learning should also draw on a wide range of research approaches, which may stem from psychology, sociology, education, or information science, to name a few. Approaches such as critical-incident technique, grounded theory, ethnography, surveys, case studies, phenomenography, and others will all make a contribution. Like earlier information-literacy research, informed learning research will identify different research objects, such as skills and behaviors, experience, or mental models. Similarly, informed learning research will explore different paradigms, for example, constructivism, constitutionalism, social constructionism, cognitivism, or critical theory (Bruce, 2000).

Research into informed learning could also demonstrate the teaching–research nexus in action. This may take the form of teachers choosing to research their own practice, including the development of classroom applications. Or it may take the form of investigations and theorization at different levels about information literacy, learning, and the interrelation between them.

Important questions that are open to investigation, and around which work has already begun, as I demonstrated in earlier chapters, include these:

- How do people use information to learn? What is their experience of informed learning in the academy, the workplace, and the community?
- What is the character of informed learning in different disciplines?
- What are the information practices that enable ongoing learning in the work of the different professions?
- What are the information practices that underpin the many disciplines being taught and learned?

- What are the forms of information engaged with and how are they used?

These questions open up the space for an informed learning research agenda, which I sketch below.

Establishing a Research Agenda

The informed learning research agenda should be seen as practical and real—it is about real people, doing real things in real-life contexts. To achieve this, we must bring together a research community that is ready to cross boundaries and forge relationships with other groups.

The following summary of recommendations for information-literacy research, from the Prague Meeting of Experts (Thompson, 2003), reveals the potential breadth of the research agenda. Each of these recommendations could be taken up under the informed learning research banner, as information literacy is a key element of informed learning.

Education and Learning
- Investigate the character of information literacy in different environments and organizations such as public and proprietary environments, oral learning communities, digital environments, and professional and community contexts.

National Case Studies
- Research existing technology, relationships between information literacy and business, and possible benefits to communities.
- Identify those with the power to act on government initiatives.

People, Culture, and Health
- Identify existing research, and create a database of studies, results, and best practice.
- Establish an interdisciplinary research council and funding for research.

Economic Development
- Identify the impact of information literacy on economic development, including cost benefit or value analysis of

workplace programs.
- Establish the relationship between information literacy and effective knowledge management.

Policy and Information Literacy
- Identify and collect research relating to the impact of information literacy.
- Compare the results of programs with and without information literacy policies.
- Develop and undertake coordinated and systematic cross-sectoral, comparative, longitudinal research projects.

The informed learning research agenda is broader than the information literacy research agenda. Taking into account the directions proposed above, researchers should target questions around
- people's experience of informed learning;
- teaching and learning for informed learning;
- information practices;
- informed learning in the workplace;
- informed learning in the research community;
- what constitutes information and how it is experienced.

An important step forward would be to establish what other research has already been conducted in different domains that may inform these areas.

Researching People's Experience of Informed Learning
We need to deepen our understanding of the character of informed learning in different spaces and of how informed learning can be enhanced. How can we, at the same time, make it possible for people to be better information users and better learners in a discipline area, or indeed across disciplines? We are only beginning to uncover people's experiences in this area, not only in traditional learning spaces, but also in the context of evolving technologies. We need to continue to understand the character of information literacy as experienced, as well as answering specific questions that are more measurable. The answering of measurable questions typically belongs to a more mature field, while here we are still working at exploring, investigating, and uncovering the phenomenon—an important precursor to further research development.

Directions for future research may include:

- researchers' experiences of informed learning;
- discipline experts' experiences of informed learning;
- students' experiences of informed learning;
- professional experiences of informed learning.

We need to understand the informed learning experiences of individuals and groups. We must also investigate the question of the character of informed learning in virtual space. For example, what does it mean to be an informed learner in Second Life? What does that experience look like? A major gap in our present understanding exists around questions of the experienced nature of knowledge, information, information literacy, and informed learning in different cultures.

Researching Teaching and Learning for Informed Learning
We need to understand better what it means to teach and learn for informed learning. How can we simultaneously help students become more information-literate and deepen their understanding of their field so that it is experienced as fully as possible?

- How do students experience learning information literacy and becoming informed learners?
- How do teachers experience teaching information literacy and bringing about informed learning?
- How do different ways of using information to learn influence learning outcomes?
- How can we enable students to adopt those ways of using information that are associated with the desired learning outcomes?

To achieve this, we need to understand more about the relationship between information use and learning, both across and within disciplines. We need to investigate how best to teach, how best to help students learn; strategies need to be developed and evaluation frameworks proposed. We need to explore how to draw on outcomes from other parts of the research agenda to help students learn.

The three critical elements in becoming an informed learner are the foundation stones of teaching and learning for informed learning:

- experiencing the different ways of using information to learn (learning)

- reflecting on experience (being aware of learning)
- applying the experience to novel contexts (transfer of learning)

Each of these involves using information and learning something, whether this be art, physics, dance, engineering, or computer science. How each of these may be best taken forward is also in need of systematic investigation.

Researching Information Practices

Academic and professional information practices reflect the idiosyncrasies of individual disciplines and professions. The importance of disciplinary contextualization when foregrounding information use in learning has been recently highlighted by the work of Sheila Webber, Bill Johnston, and Stuart Boon, and also by Vesa Kautto and Sanna Talja. Webber, Boon, and Johnston (2007) have commenced the process of establishing the character of information literacy and information-literacy pedagogy in specific disciplines. Kautto and Talja (2007) have explored the process of learning to evaluate scholarly literature in discipline contexts. We need to reopen critical questions such as:

- What are the information practices that underpin the many disciplines being taught and learned?
- What are the information practices that enable ongoing learning in different professions and disciplines? How are they experienced?
- What are the information practices that enable people to learn with and from each other? How are they experienced?

There are many examples of investigations into the ways in which different professions, disciplines, and community groups interact with information. While they may not target significant differences in experience, they do provide rich pictures of information-seeking and information-use activity in different professional or discipline contexts.

Considerable work remains to be done in identifying the important information practices in specific disciplines, professions, and other contexts.

Researching Informed Learning in the Community

Informed learning in the community is the most under-researched aspect of the academic, workplace, and community triangle. Like community information-literacy research, the informed learning research agenda must represent the disenfranchised, as well as investigating important community issues and concerns, such as:

- The experience of informed learning in different community contexts, such as health; finances; the environment; rural, urban, or indigenous communities; including oral learning and e-communities. We need to investigate questions such as:
  — Does the character of informed learning differ in specific contexts? Is it supported by forms of information literacy that also differ in specific contexts (e.g., Can we talk of health information literacy, financial information literacy, etc.)? How do we identify the relevant contexts?
  — What motivates people to walk the informed learning path?
- Strategies for building communities of informed learners:
  — How do we identify appropriate strategies for enabling informed learning (within a high-tech context) across the community as people increasingly need to deal with finance, education, health, politics, and other issues online?
  — How do we identify appropriate strategies to bring the informational needs and contexts of disempowered groups to the fore?

Researching Informed Learning in the Workplace

How do people use information to learn in the workplace? Research interest in this area is emerging. Progress in this direction will benefit from increased interaction with research into workplace learning and also research into people's use of technology at work. Progressing research in this area also requires us to distinguish between researching informed learning in the workplace and researching the professional experiences of information literacy. Researching the workplace differs from researching professional experience in that workplaces are bound up with organizational culture and may bring people with different types of expertise together. For example, we could research informed learning among lawyers as a professional group, or we could research informed learning in a legal firm as a workplace. We could research informed learning among teachers as a professional group, or we could research informed learning in a school as a workplace. We could research informed learning among nurses as a professional group, or we could research informed learning in a hospital as a workplace.

Some of the questions to ask include:

- What does it mean to be an informed learner at work?
- How can workplaces support informed learning?
- What does informed learning look like in different workplaces? How is it experienced in airports, hospitals, restaurants, schools, department stores, and hotels, to name a few?

Researching What Constitutes Information and How It Is Experienced
A vital element of the informed learning agenda is the question of what constitutes information in different settings or contexts, in different disciplines, professions, cultures, and communities. We need to investigate and uncover the forms of information important to these communities and to investigate the different ways in which that information might appear in different communities. Even in the academic world, for example, nontextual information is rarely recognized as information.

Some of the questions to ask include:

- What constitutes information in different contexts? What appears as information, and how does that information appear?
- What are the different forms of information engaged with? How are they used?

We should not impose the view of information and the kinds of information established by the developed world universally; we need to recognize and make possible the use of information that is meaningful in other contexts. Joan Challinor (in Thompson, 2003, p. 25) points towards indigenous art, stories, folk medicine, oral histories, religions, cultures—indigenous knowledge of all kinds—as a small selection of examples that are not commonly considered information.

Researching Informed Learning in the Research Community
Informed learning in the research community is a potentially fruitful and presently much under-researched area.

- What is the nature of the experience of informed learning in the research community? How does that experience differ, across and within disciplines or fields of study?

- What is the character of the relationship between ways of seeing research and information use?
- What is the character of the relationship between ways of seeing research objects and information use in that field?
- Do different ways of seeing research influence information use?
- Do different ways of experiencing information use influence research outcomes?
- What are the different information practices that researchers engage in?
- Is there a connection between how research is experienced and how researchers' information practices are experienced?
- How can we help research students learn these research practices?
- What forms does information take in different disciplines? What are the different ways in which it appears to researchers?

More specific questions related to learning practices could also be asked. For example:

- How do ways of seeing literature reviews, information, or relevance influence research outcomes?
- How do students experience the scope of the literature review in different phases of their project?

What Is Required to Take This Agenda Forward?
First, We Need to Bring Multiple Lenses to Our Research
I have found while working with academics and librarians in many disciplines that as academics, we are not used to looking at learning through an information lens, and as librarians, we are not used to looking at information use through a learning lens. This observation comes from my own experience of working as a member of both groups over the years, as well as from working closely with both groups on developing the information-literacy agenda.

If we are to research how the experience of information use influences learning or how the experience of learning influences information use, as well as investigating how each informs the other, we need to bring the learning lens, the information lens, and discipline and professional lenses to bear upon our work.

Second, We Need to Attend Deeply to Using Information to Learn

We still pay far more attention to information seeking and gathering than using information for learning, despite our stated interest in information literacy. We need to understand what it means to think about using information and learning simultaneously. We need to explore the learning that is happening as people seek and gather. Using information to learn includes information seeking and gathering, as well as extending beyond. We need to explore the interrelation between information use and learning.

Third, We Need Partnerships

Beyond the immediate advocates for information literacy, usually information or learning specialists, we need a broader range of partners, including academics from all disciplines and business, government, and community leaders to work together in establishing, funding, and taking forward the agenda. In addition, efforts must be made to establish links with the priorities of research-funding bodies or to influence those priorities to more readily recognize the role of informed learning research.

We also need to remember that all sectors of the community are partners, and equal partners, in the quest for an informed society. We need to increase the ways in which it is possible for people to communicate with each other around informed learning issues. All our strategies for electronic communication cannot take the place of meeting each other face-to-face and engaging with important directions and concerns.

Fourth, We Need to Broaden Our Cross-Sectoral Engagement

We need to broaden our interest to take in using information to learn beyond formal educational arenas. By far the majority of interest in information literacy is still in formal educational arenas. The emphasis on lifelong learning in the knowledge society should have changed this by now, but it has not. The inclusion of workplace and community sectors in the conversation is still too limited.

Fifth, We Need to Become Advocates for the Disempowered
As we focus on information literacy, we are confronted with the need to continue to deal with poor levels of basic literacy in society generally and in specific parts of the world. There are still too many people who cannot begin to consider taking advantage of the higher-order capabilities on offer, when reading and writing are still a challenge. We are easily lured into believing that information and technology literacy provide solutions to deep problems and perhaps forget that in every situation, not everyone is capable of taking advantage of the solutions we offer. We need to think and act upon questions like these: *How can we bridge the reality of today and possible futures? How can we work where we are to help people move into the possibilities of tomorrow? How can we bring about societies and people that are empowered politically, socially, and economically?*

References

Bowden, J., & Marton, F. (1998). *The university of learning: Beyond quality and competence in higher education.* London: Kogan Page.

Bruce, C. S. (2000). Information literacy research: Dimensions of an emerging collective consciousness. *Australian Academic and Research Libraries, 31*(2), 91–109.

Kautto, V., & Talja, S. (2007). Disciplinary socialization: Learning to evaluate the quality of scholarly literature. *Advances in Library Administration and Organization 25,* 33–59.

Kirk, J. (2004). Tumble dryers and juggernauts: Information use processes in organizations. In *Lifelong learning: Whose responsibility and what is your contribution? Refereed papers from the 3rd Lifelong Learning conference, Yeppoon, Australia, 13–16 June 2004,* pp. 192–197. http://lifelonglearning.cqu.edu.au/2004/papers

Limberg, L., & Folkesson, L. (2006). Information seeking, didactics and learning (IDOL). Summary in English. In Undervisning i informationssökning. Slutrapport från projektet Informationssökning, didaktik och lärande (IDOL). [Teaching information seeking. Final report from the project Information seeking, didactics and learning.] (pp. 8–10). Borås, Sweden: Valfrid. [Summary also available at http://www.hb.se/bhs/personal/lol/engsum.pdf]

Marton, F., & Booth, S. (1997). *Learning and awareness.* Mahwah, NJ: Erlbaum.

Marton, F., & Tsui, A. B. M. (2004). *Classroom discourse and the space of learning.* Mahwah, NJ: Erlbaum.

Thompson, S. (2003). The information literacy meeting of experts. Prague the Czech Republic, Sept 20–23, 2003. Report of a meeting sponsored by the U.S. National Commission on Libraries and Information Science (NCLIS) and the National Forum for Information Literacy (NFIL) with the support of UNESCO. Available at: http://www.nclis.gov/libinter/infolitconf&meet/post-infolitconf&meet/FinalReportPrague.pdf (accessed: April 20, 2007).

Printed in the United States
141622LV00007B/6/P

9 780838 984895